The Gift of GRIEF

For Those Who Grieve...

...and a Call to the Church to Come Alongside Them

MARCIA WEIR

The Gift of Grief by Marcia Weir

© 2025 Marcia Weir

ISBN 9781896213187   Print Edition 2025

ISBN 9781896213194   E-book Edition 2025

Scripture taken from the New King James Version®. Copyright © 1982 by Thomas Nelson. Used by permission. All rights reserved.

Scripture quotations taken from the (NASB®) New American Standard Bible®, Copyright ©1960,1971, 1977 by The Lockman Foundation. Used by permission All rights reserved. lockman.org

All rights reserved. No part of this publication may be reproduced, stored in a retrieval system, or transmitted in any form or by any means without prior permission of the copyright owner.

Published in Canada by ByDesign Media, Paris, Ontario, Canada
www.bydesignmedia.ca
Cover by Diane Roblin-Lee

Contents

Disclaimer — 5
Dedication — 7
Acknowledgments — 9
Foreword — 15
Ron's Note — 16
Prologue — 17
Introduction — 21

Part One – Grief: The Unwelcome Guest — 27
Chapter 1 – The Club I Never Wanted to Join — 29
Chapter 2 – What is Grief? — 39
Chapter 3 – Are There Really Five Stages to Grief? — 49
Chapter 4 – How Do You Grieve? — 55

Part Two – Grief: The Thief — 61
Chapter 5 – Lest We Forget — 63
Chapter 6 – There's Good and Bad Anger — 69
Chapter 7 – Regrets and Guilt; Forgiveness and Grace — 85
Chapter 8 – Irreplaceable Memories — 95
Chapter 9 – The First Year – Dates in Memoriam — 105
Chapter 10 – When You Lose a Child — 115

Part Three – Grief: The Teacher — 125
Chapter 11 – Change is Inevitable — 127
Chapter 12 – Nothing New About My 'New Normal' — 135
Chapter 13 – Help! What Do I Say? — 145
Chapter 14 – I Shouldn't Have Said That! — 153

Part Four – Grief: The Gift — 161
Chapter 15 – God's Call to the Church — 163
Chapter 16 – A Few Words to My Fellow Grievers — 179
Chapter 17 – A Heart of Gratitude — 187
Chapter 18 – Where Do We Go From Here? — 193

Epilogue — 197
Appendix A — 203
Appendix B — 207
Notes — 208

Disclaimer

The following pages have been written with a twofold purpose – first, to comfort and encourage those in the grieving community with the same comfort I have received and found to be helpful; and second, to raise awareness and help the Body of Christ, the Church, understand how desperately we need your ongoing love and support as we walk this journey. It is a lengthy walk of time and commitment with the hurting and broken-hearted.

I am not a counsellor, a doctor, medical or mental healthcare professional, clergy, theologian or educator of any sort. I do not give or suggest any form of medical advice or prescribe any form of treatment. I quote from those who are recognized and respected as experts in the various fields and who have passed on their knowledge to all of us through their writings as a means of sharing their expertise on the various subjects.

Dedication

This book is lovingly dedicated to my late husband, Ron Weir, with gratitude to God for blessing my life with you for 41 years of marriage. I miss so many things about you, most of all your presence, but I do not grieve as one without hope. My hope is in Jesus who has promised that we will be reunited on that final day. May His Name be glorified through the writing and purpose of this book. May it be a tribute to your life and may the Church understand how much the grieving community needs them to walk with us as we journey through the painful valley of death, suffering, and loss.

Acknowledgments

If all of us were given the opportunity to write a book on any topic of our choosing, I would venture to say very few would choose the topic of grief. It is not a topic that people readily gravitate toward. It is quite the opposite. People have an aversion to the suffering we will experience as a result of grief, death and loss, but it is something that touches all of us at various points in our lives. It can't be avoided. Such has been the case in my own life. It came out of nowhere. I never anticipated it, but I felt compelled to write about it.

Being a novice at this special skill of writing requires having gifted and knowledgeable people around me to help me through the process. I am so indebted to my publisher, Diane Roblin-(Lee) Rutledge of byDesign Media. I am so aware that it was God's hand that led me to you, Diane. I remember our first conversation. You were in Mexico, writing another book. Even amid your busy schedule, you were willing to hear my story and take me on.

Thank you for the guidance, advice, encouragement and prayers you have shared with me in this part of my grief journey. You recognized the need and necessity of this book. You caught the vision. Your expertise, encouragement, support, and patience have been such a blessing and gift to me. Thank you so much.

To Melanie Swackhammer, thank you for your editorial skills in helping to make this a book worthy of reading and ministering to those for whom it is intended. I learned a lot about contractions. *(wink)*

To my sister, Jeanne Best, an author in her own right—you offered to do a 'pre-edit edit' upon learning that I was writing this book. Not everyone gets an offer like that! I have learned from your critiquing (in love) of the pages and pages you read and made notes on to help me as I took this step of faith. You were so right when you said, *"You have written your heart. Now it's time to write the book."* You have walked beside me every step of the way. You and Jim have been with me in the darkest days of my life and since that time, you have never left my side. I am so blessed to have you in my life. What a gift you are to me! I love you so much.

To my dearest friend, Carrie Fleetwood, I am indebted to you for your support and for allowing me to 'tap into' your expertise as a psychotherapist. I wanted to make sure what I was conveying wasn't merely my perspective, but held validity concerning specific topics I was including in this book. I am so blessed by the 50 plus years that we have been friends. We have experienced the joys of life (our children and grandkids) and sorrows of loss in each other's life (your mother, my parents, and Ron). Your expertise and perspective have been invaluable to me. Your support throughout the writing of this book, and checking in to see how I was coping with my grief after Ron passed away has been a gift to me. Thank you, dear friend. I love you.

To my dear friend and colleague from Peoples Christian Academy days—Vanessa Peart - thank you for taking time out of your hectic teaching and family schedule to read the manuscript and use your skills to show me where I could make improvements. Your encouragement and seeing the vision for this book in ministering to those in pain was not just timely, but a reinforcement of the Lord's direction. Thank you. You have blessed me richly.

To Lori Penrice and Darlene Moran—I don't believe there are better GriefShare facilitators! You are such an amazing team! God has blessed you both with such wisdom and compassion in coming alongside those of us going through the devastation of death, suffering, and loss. It was through your leadership, support, and encouragement in the GriefShare ministry, and to me personally, that confirmed God's direction in my life to become a facilitator. Thank you for the time you faithfully invest in coming alongside those who grieve.

To Pastor Warren Morris—your ministry to me as I tried to navigate my way through the shock and devastation of losing Ron truly blessed my life. From that first phone call I received in Nova Scotia to the conversations we have subsequently shared about ministering to the bereaved, have helped to confirm God's direction for ministry in this next chapter of my life. Your encouragement as I wrote this book was such a blessing. God has definitely given you a pastor's heart in reaching out to the hurting and wounded. Thank you so much.

To those of you who were willing to share your stories of grief and sorrow with me so that I could share them with those who read this book—you are a big part of the ministry of these pages to the broken and wounded, giving them hope amid the darkest days of their lives. You opened your hearts and shared your pain so that others could identify with you and recognize that they don't have to walk alone. Thank you for your resilience and example of trust in a loving God when nothing made any sense during the most painful experiences anyone can have.

To all those who encouraged me along the way, believing this book needed to be written, supporting me every step of the way through words of encouragement and prayers—thank you. You have been my cheerleaders. I am so grateful for each of you—my dear mentor for over 45 years, Gerry Clemenger-Nelson, Carrie Fleetwood, Carol Tai, Rob and Myrna Gowing, Andy Tesluk, Dr. Karen Smith, Pauline Hoskins, Dr. Michael

(Mike) Shapiro, Gary Roe, Nadia Tymciw, Lynette Wells, Shaun Lapenskie, Jennifer Lee, Brenda Ibbitson, Marilyn Shewfelt, and Linda Pequegnat. I want to give a special acknowledgment to my dear friend, Cary Zigelstein. He has now moved on to Glory but was my encourager through a difficult knee replacement, then through Ron's death, and now the writing of this book, while he himself was fighting cancer. We will meet again in the morning, my friend. To those in my condo building who knew the book was being written, you too, cheered me on. *(And yes, Jim–the book is finally here!)*

But there are four people I owe everything to—my daughters, Shauna and Brittany, and their husbands (my 'sons') Brandon and Dave. You kids mean the absolute world to me. I'm indebted to the Lord for blessing my life with you. We have laughed and cried together. We've grieved deeply together, as we've walk this journey of profound sorrow, pain, and loss. Your constant encouragement of me writing this book helped to keep me going. Dad/Ron will always hold a special place in each of our hearts that will never be filled by another. I want to add a special thank you to Dave for the hours you spent helping me with my 'computer skills'. I think I officially proved that technology is not my strong point and if something can go wrong, chances are, I helped make it happen! And although she is only a toddler, my adorable granddaughter, Haddie, on more than one occasion helped to brighten my days, lift my spirits, and bring a smile to my face amid my tears with her kisses and *"I love ooo's"*, that she shared with her Mimi on FaceTime. I thank God for each of you, and I love you 'bigger than the sky.'

However, the greatest debt of gratitude I owe is to my Lord Jesus Christ. He has been faithful to His Word to take good care of me. He confirmed that He had a purpose for me writing this book. He challenged me to step out in faith once again, believing and trusting this was His plan for my life, and all He asked was that I be obedient and trust Him for that which I couldn't see. I have learned lessons that could only be learned during the darkest nights of my soul. Most of all, I have learned that God *never* wastes our experiences no matter how heartbreaking they may be. He has taught me that the *'gift'* of grief truly is a gift to be sought after because it leads us to the very heart of God. For that, I am eternally grateful.

Foreword

In this concise and powerful book, *The Gift of Grief,* Marcia masterfully takes us with her into her journey of loss and grief. With vulnerability she invites us into lessons she's learned for herself and through listening to others. Her compassionate heart guides the grieving to turn our eyes to Scripture and our loving God, who in our grief provides ultimate comfort and hope. She shares her discovery that grief can actually be a gift as we walk with God in it.

With insight borne through personal loss, Marcia invites the Church to leave fear behind and gives practical examples of how to learn, change, and engage with those who have been crushed by inevitable loss and grief.

We highly commend this book to all, for grief is a part of life.

Gerald and Dorothy Hogenbirk
Former Regional Directors for the C&MA in Europe, Middle East, Central Asia and the Arabian Peninsula

*A note from my husband, Ron,
prior to his passing.*

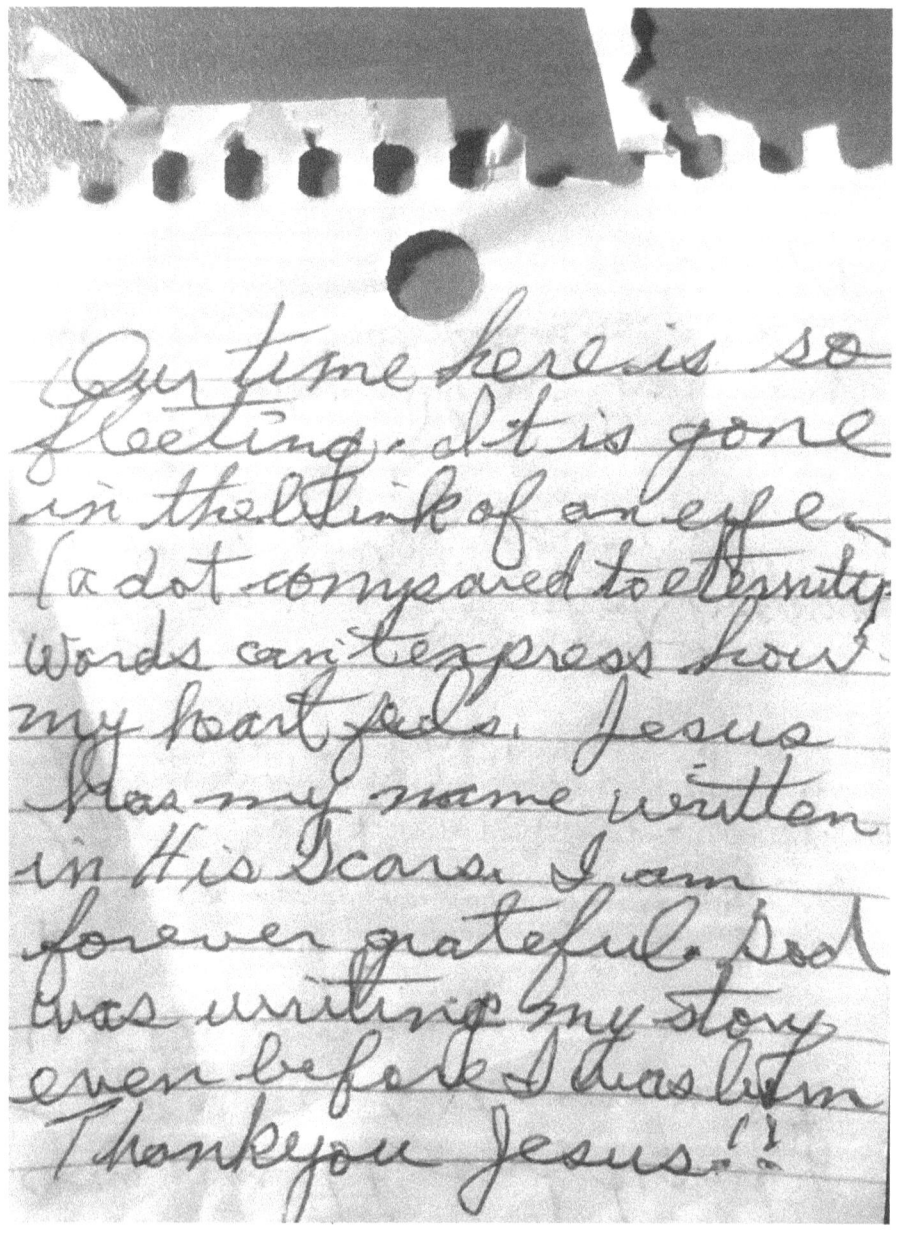

The Gift of Grief

Prologue

Even to your old age, I shall be the same,
And even to your greying years I shall bear you!
I have done it, and I shall carry you;
And I shall bear you, and I shall deliver you.[1]

God never wastes our experiences.

When I led Women's Ministries in the church, how many times did I share those five words with women who were facing challenges and difficulties? I tried to encourage them with the truth that God was big enough to handle the unwanted events that unexpectedly assaulted their lives. Here I was again sharing those words—this time with my son-in-law as he drove me to the airport. Dave lost his management job six weeks before he was to marry our younger daughter, Brittany. He had worked for fourteen years for this company and was good at what he did. When cuts were made, he was assured that his job was secure. Unfortunately, that was not the case. It was a shock! It was

---

1. Isaiah 46:4 NASB.

devastating! It was numbing! It was life changing! How did this happen? Why did it happen? It didn't make sense and it was like an arrow to his heart. He wasn't ready for this! Now what?

Little did I know that two months after Dave and Brittany's wedding, I too would experience the greatest loss of my life. My husband of 41 years died on the operating table. I wasn't prepared for this! It was a shock! It was devastating! It was numbing! It was life changing! I was left asking the same questions. How did this happen? Why did it happen? It didn't make sense and it was like an arrow to my heart. Now what? Those five words were going to have a greater impact on my life than I could've ever imagined.

The first night that I was alone, I cried out to God, asking Him how I would be able to carry on by myself. I had depended on Ron for so many things. Just ten months earlier, he was my support through a difficult knee replacement. When I got home from the hospital, he looked after everything. I couldn't get in and out of bed without his help. For four months he applied ice packs every two to three hours, day and night. He assisted me with the exercises, took me to physiotherapy appointments and follow-up appointments with the surgeon in Markham. He cooked, cleaned, and did the grocery shopping because I was unable to do any of those things. As I faced the possibility of a second knee replacement, I wondered how I would manage without him. He was my hands and feet. He was my provider and encourager. I had a million questions about what my life would be like without him. I worried about what would happen to my daughters if something happened to me. I was consumed with these fears, and in the midst of my overwhelming distress, I felt the Lord impress His words upon my mind, *"I will take good care of you."* But even then, I asked, *"How?"*

The Lord has been true to His word to me. He's taken good care of me through my family and through people I least expected—my financial adviser, my tax accountant, my physiotherapist, my contractor, my mechanic, my real estate agent, to name only a few. Interestingly, they've expressed the same care and encouragement— *"I will take good care of you."* They're unaware of how God impressed these words on my mind and heart that first night without Ron.

I thank God for His faithfulness to me every day. He's encouraged me and taken good care of me through them. He's been teaching me lessons in gratitude, lessons in trust, and lessons in seeing the needs of others who are walking through this devastatingly lonely valley of death and loss. I want to help them however I can. These lessons in gratitude, trust, and helping others in their darkest hours, have helped bring healing in my own journey of grief and God is glorified.

Every page of this book is covered with tears. Tears of gratitude, tears of regret, and tears of deep sadness. There have been tears of intense loneliness now that Ron's gone, tears that express heartfelt prayers, and most of all, tears of love. Tears not only for Ron, but for the One who is faithful to His Word. Because He is true to His Word, He can be trusted. He *never* wastes our experiences.

The Gift of Grief

Introduction

The Spirit of the Lord is upon Me,
Because the Lord has anointed Me
To preach good tidings to the poor;
He has sent Me to heal the brokenhearted, ...
To comfort all who mourn ...[2]

"Give yourself the gift of grief."

These were the words spoken to me in the Walmart parking lot a week after I buried my husband. My shopping cart had started to roll toward an oncoming car. When I realized what was happening, I managed to rescue it within an inch or two of hitting the car. I burst into tears. I couldn't handle it anymore. I was exhausted and my emotions were frazzled. A man in his 40's was watching the whole thing from about five cars down the row. Perhaps he thought he was about to witness an accident.

---

2. Isaiah 61: 1-2 NKJV.

He yelled out to me, *"Great save!"* He saw me crying and came over to ask if I was okay. I told him, *"No, my husband died two weeks ago."* I was expecting the typical, *"Oh, I'm sorry,"* followed by watching him try to get away from an awkward moment. However, this man was different. His mannerisms and voice were kind. He said he was sorry and then asked if he could say something to me. I hesitatingly said, *"Yes."* He proceeded to tell me not to let anyone say how long I should grieve—that everyone grieves differently and there is no set time frame for how long grief lasts. He told me to take the time to grieve. The words, *"Give yourself the gift of grief,"* struck a chord in my heart. I got in my car and sat there crying for ten minutes. To this day, I can't help but wonder if this was an angel in disguise.

"Give yourself the gift of grief." To me that was an oxymoron. Grief. Even the very word itself stirs up uncomfortable feelings. When I checked various dictionaries and thesauruses, they all used the same or similar words to describe grief—words like agony, suffering, loss, overwhelming sadness, anguish, pain, disorientation, heartbroken, intense sorrow, misery, distress, despair, bereavement, lament, and mourning.

However, the one word that I did **not** find to describe grief was "gift." No one thinks of grief as a gift. No one loves grief. We abhor it! We hate it! Grief is looked upon as an enemy and a thief. It robs us of our happiness and brings loneliness and sadness in its wake. How could anyone possibly think of it as a gift? It's relentless in its waves and triggers—prompting tears when we feel there are no more tears to cry. It causes our eyes to sting! It touches the depths of our soul, a place we have never visited before. We don't want to go there! It's excruciating! It haunts us during the midnight hours, robbing us of the sleep of which we are already so deprived. Many have likened it to hell, so surely it can't be called a *gift!*

A gift is something we receive with a sense of happiness, a feeling of acceptance, warmth, and love. It's an expression of generosity from one person to another. It says, *"I appreciate you." "I like you." "I love you." "You're special."* So how could anyone say grief was a *gift?* Grief is the furthest thing from a gift… Or is it?

I don't profess to be an author, a teacher, a pastor, or a counsellor. I'm a mom, a grandmother, a daughter, a sister, an aunt, a friend—and now… a widow. Most of what I've been learning from this journey of grief, many others have experienced and written about already. However, before I met that stranger in the parking lot, I had never heard anyone refer to grief as a gift.

One thing of which I became acutely aware at the onset of my journey, is how important it is for us, the Church, as a whole, to recognize the valuable and significant role that is ours in addressing the ongoing needs of those who are grieving. We need to understand how much we are needed to come alongside those experiencing the darkest days of their lives. It is a labour of love and a commitment of time. Many admit they often struggle to know what to say and how to comfort those who are grieving.

What do you say to parents who've lost a child to cancer or some other dreaded disease? What do you say to someone whose parent or spouse has been kidnapped by Alzheimer's and no longer recognizes you, but instead greets you with a blank stare and silence? What do you do to come alongside a family who has lost a loved one to the tragedy of suicide? How do you come alongside a family whose son was murdered because he happened to be in the wrong place at the wrong time? How do you comfort a couple who've lost their first baby during childbirth because, upon delivery, the cord was wrapped around the baby's neck? How do you support someone whose entire family was wiped out by a drunk driver, a house fire or any other kind of devastating catastrophe?

Grief is not just related to a physical death. There are those who experience grief through the devastating loss of a job, their home, their spouse through separation and divorce, their reputation, their independence due to a terminal illness or an accident, or the loss of a close friendship they highly valued, but was suddenly broken off without explanation.

The purpose of this book is to challenge us to come alongside those going through deep pain and loss and be willing to learn how to minister to the grieving among us—to be part of *the gift of grief*. In order to do that, we need to hear their experiences. We need to try to see their pain through their eyes. It is my prayer that by sharing some of my personal pain, as well as the pain of others, we will be encouraged to recognize how desperately needed and important it is to walk with those who are part of the community of grievers in our churches and communities.

You're probably familiar with the old adage that we never truly understand what someone else is going through until we walk in their shoes. In other words, it isn't until we put ourselves in someone else's situation that we can begin to gain a small understanding of what they are going through. It means to see something from someone else's perspective. It means to have empathy for what they're experiencing. For those around us who are experiencing the profound pain of grief, it means listening to what they're saying so we can try to gain even a hint of the depth of their suffering. It means being willing to shed our preconceived ideas of what we think about grief and stand with those who have to forge their way through the challenges and wounds of loss. How long should they grieve? When should they get involved in the ministry of the church? Why do we assume they should be *moving on* or *getting on with their lives*? Who among us has the authority to make those decisions on their behalf?

So I ask you: Are *we* willing to learn? Are *we* willing to change our thinking? Are *we* willing to invest time and love in the lives of those who have no hope and feel like their lives have been destroyed? Very simply put: Are *we* willing to be the ones who need to change? If the answer is yes, I invite you to read on.

Part One

GRIEF

The Unwelcome Guest

The Gift of Grief

Chapter One

The Club I Never Wanted to Join

The Lord is near to the brokenhearted,
And saves those who are crushed in spirit.[3]

When I look back, it was a whirlwind three weeks. Ron had started commenting on how frustrated he was about getting winded climbing stairs. I didn't think much of it at the time because *I* get winded doing stairs! However, when he began complaining of a tightness in his chest, I urged him to make an appointment with our family doctor. He called and made the appointment, but the soonest he could get in was on November 27th, which was three weeks away. By Monday, November 20th, he was becoming more concerned, so he decided to go to a walk-in clinic to get the second opinion first.

When he came home, I asked how the appointment went. The doctor on-call said his blood pressure was high and gave him a prescription for blood pressure medication and told him to take

---

3. Psalm 34:18   NASB.

ASAs. I asked what his blood pressure reading was and he said, *"176/105."* I was stunned! My first response was, *"And they didn't tell you to go to the ER immediately?"* Apparently not. He took the medication and ate dinner. At 9:30 pm, two hours later, he asked me to call 911—he needed to go to the ER.

The firemen and paramedics arrived in minutes. By this time, Ron was getting quite agitated about how he was feeling. The paramedics had to tell him three times to sit still, stop lifting his arm, and to stop talking as they tried to get a read on the test they were performing. It was obvious that he was totally oblivious to how worked up he was. The fireman commented on how excited he was. They said they were taking him to the ER because his blood pressure was now 190/110. I was instructed to wait at home. Ron was to call me and let me know when I should come to pick him up. I waited, but no call came.

When I called Tuesday morning at 6:30 am, they said he had just been admitted but was still in the ER. They had him on meds and were doing more tests, but he was still experiencing chest pain. The nurse commented that for the amount of meds he was on he shouldn't be able to feel anything, but he did, so they up-ed them. They couldn't perform the angiogram so they did an echocardiogram instead. His arteries were 95 and 99% blocked. He had CAD—coronary artery disease—and we had no idea. This came as a huge surprise because Ron was not overweight. He loved the outdoors and worked seasonally at a golf course cutting greens. He went on two to three walks every day, and for the most part we tried to eat healthy.

Our younger daughter, Brittany, took time off work and came to see her dad that afternoon. She was going to be flying to Halifax the next day to meet her new niece—our first grandchild. She took a picture, as she always did, with her dad before she left. Little did we know this would be the last picture taken of Ron on this side of Glory.

By Wednesday morning—the following day—the doctors said they were making arrangements for him to be transferred to Southlake Hospital in Newmarket, the heart hospital. I was told it might take a week before they could get a surgery date and a bed there. I told them I didn't want him coming home because I had no idea what to do for him. They assured me that he was being kept in the hospital and they were watching him closely. By that afternoon, we received word that Southlake had juggled their schedule and Ron would be transported on Thursday, the next day. It was clear they understood the urgency, as his surgery was scheduled for 7:00 am Friday morning.

The transport came on Thursday at noon to take Ron to Southlake. Just before they started to wheel him down to the elevator, he looked at me and said, *"I love you, Sweetie."* I told him I loved him, too. It was our last kiss and hug. As I look back on that, I can't help but feel he had some kind of premonition that he might not make it. It was a very intense hug and kiss. He knew

I was going to be following them down to Southlake, but I never got to see him again. They were preparing him for surgery, so I drove home.

My sister Jeanne drove me down the next morning to be there while the surgery was taking place. Brittany's husband, Dave, joined us, and we waited to hear from the surgeon. At 12 noon, the surgeon came to the waiting room and said the surgery had been successful and Ron's heart was good. They had to do a triple bypass. We could see him, but needed to realize that he was still sedated and wouldn't know we were there. I steeled myself for what I might see. A cardiac nurse at the Royal Victoria Regional Health Centre in Barrie warned me, *"He won't look good after the surgery. He will be grey. Don't be shocked by that."* When Dave and I went in, Ron was under a warming blanket. The first thing I said to Dave was, *"He looks good!"* He had all his colour and wasn't grey at all. Because of the good report and because he was going to be sedated for hours, we decided to go home. They said they were going to take the breathing tube out at 4:00 pm and to call around 4:15 pm for an update.

When I called for the update, the nurse said to call back in an hour because the doctor was working with a patient. I never thought anything of it and called again an hour later. Again, I was told that the doctor was still working with the patient and that he would call me. When I got off the phone, I realized the patient they were referring to was Ron! The surgeon called me at 5:40

pm and began with the words, *"I'm sorry, Mrs. Weir. Two of the three bypasses have failed. We are putting an emergency team together right now and we will be taking him back to surgery tonight at 9:30 pm."* My head was spinning! He said they don't like to do this, but if they didn't operate, Ron would die. He then said I needed to know that the risks were high and that he might not survive the surgery. While he was speaking with me, Ron was having another heart attack. I couldn't process the information I had been given. This is the heart hospital! They do hundreds of successful bypass surgeries every year. They said his heart was good. How can this be? Were they talking about *my* Ron or did they have him confused with another patient?

    Jeanne and Jim drove me back to Southlake for the 9:30 pm surgery, and Dave met us in the waiting room once again. For some reason, it never crossed my mind that Ron wouldn't make it. Friends and family were praying. I honestly thought he would come through it. At 1:00 am, the surgeon came out and said he was sorry. He then went on to say that Ron was on life support and that we could go in to see him in a few minutes. My sister said she could see that I didn't understand what the surgeon was saying. I didn't know he was saying Ron was gone. Because Ron was on a ventilator after the first surgery, it stood to reason he would be on one after the second surgery. For me, it meant the same thing. The surgeon returned a few minutes later to say that the anesthesiologist had turned the life support machine off at 1:16 am. Ron was gone.

My sister told me later that they watched me go into shock. All I kept saying was, *"Oh my God! Oh my God!"* I have no recollection to this day of what transpired for the next 2.5 hours. It's as if God drew a curtain across my memory.

The next day, I told my sister I was upset because we didn't get to see him. She said, *"We did."* She said I threw myself across his chest and cried and kissed him. She said it was gut-wrenching. They got a wheelchair for me because they thought I was going to collapse. I have no memory of this. I have no memory of us calling my daughters, Shauna and Brittany, in Nova Scotia, to let them know. I don't even recall the ride home. I apparently just kept asking the same questions over and over again—*"Did he die? How did he die? When did he die? Why did he die?"* Every time I asked, Jeanne patiently repeated the answers, recognizing that I had no idea what was going on. My memory didn't resume until we walked into my condo at 3:30 am.

Jeanne said she was going to stay with me. She tried to encourage me to get some sleep, but my brain wouldn't let that happen. I couldn't sleep. This was all so surreal. I went out to the living room and sat in Ron's chair, trying to remember what happened, but to no avail. I recall thinking this was all a bad dream, that he hadn't died, and that he would be coming home in a few days. When Jeanne joined me in the living room, I asked the same questions again. She calmly gave the same answers. We eventually went back to bed, but I don't recall getting much sleep, if any at all.

The next days were a whirlwind of preparing for Ron's memorial and burial. People were surprised that I spoke at the memorial, but shock is like a buffer for our brains. It truly is a gift from God—it is His way of protecting our brain from the trauma we experience.

The preparations for a funeral and burial can leave one feeling inundated. Cemetery arrangements, funeral arrangements, burial arrangements, purchasing a casket, writing the obituary, as well as writing what I was going to say at the memorial service. There are the donation details, organizing a service, and all the preparation that goes into that. Rental and service fees, thank you notes, contacting an officiant and all others who would take part in the service. A florist, a caterer, going through a myriad of pictures, preparing a bulletin, and the list goes on. This doesn't even touch on the financial aspects that must be attended to after the funeral, like insurance policies and estate income tax preparation. I had to contact Service Canada to cancel Ron's driver's license and his health card. Credit card companies needed to be notified. There was so much to do. Yet, somehow, we got through it all. I couldn't have done it without family and their contacts.

I am still trying to come to terms with the word widow. It was okay when it applied to others, but it has been an adjustment for me. When I called dear friends who'd also lost their spouses to let them know about Ron, I would begin by saying this was a club I never wanted to join—the widows' club. It just didn't feel or sound right. Every day and everywhere I went, I was intensely aware that I was no longer a wife or part of a couple. I was now alone—single—on my own—a widow… and I hated it. I felt like I'd lost part of my identity. I used to be Ron's wife, and that was now gone. I was no longer part of a marriage. I was now the odd number sitting with other couples. I had to go for a gastroscopy procedure and the woman at Triage asked me what my marital status was. Even eleven months after Ron had died, I wasn't ready for that question and I definitely wasn't ready for my response. The word widow caught in my throat and the floodgates opened. She was very kind, but it was at that moment that I recognized that I still hadn't adjusted to my new identity, and this made my grief more overwhelming.

For a number of months after Ron's death, I had to monitor my blood pressure because the trauma I experienced had impacted it, and the doctor wanted me to keep an eye on it. The trauma of grief can do harmful things to our bodies if we aren't careful. Sometimes the pain of loss was so intense I wondered if I was going to have a heart attack myself.

When I think back on the memorial service, it was a beautiful tribute to Ron's life and to his faith in Jesus. The Gospel was clearly presented, which was my goal when I organized it. I knew he would've been pleased with the service. It was wonderful to see so many dear friends and family and feel their support in the moment. And God's gift of shock carried us through. As exhausting as the day was, I didn't want it to end because I knew the hardest days were now ahead of us. At some point, the shock would subside, the condolence cards and notes would no longer fill our mailboxes, meals brought to the family would eventually stop being delivered, and life would resume back to normal... for everyone but us.

The Gift of Grief

Chapter Two

What is Grief?

Have mercy on me, O Lord, for I am weak;
O Lord, heal me, for my bones are troubled.
My soul also is greatly troubled;...
Return, O Lord, deliver me!
O save me for Your mercies sake! ...
I am weary with my groaning;
All night long I make my bed swim;
I drench my couch with my tears.
My eye wastes away because of grief ...[4]

Without love, grief does not exist.

When I was a teenager, I worked on staff at a kids' camp. At campfires, the kids loved to sing the various camp songs. They especially loved action songs. One of their favourites was called,

---

[4]. Psalm 6:2-4, 6-7 NKJV.

"Going on a Lion Hunt." The camp leader would say the sentence and the kids would echo it. The words went like this:

"Going on a lion hunt. (Going on a lion hunt).

Gonna catch a big one. (Gonna catch a big one).

I'm not scared. (I'm not scared).

Oh, what a beautiful day. (Oh, what a beautiful day).

Oh no! (Oh no!).

Tall grass. (Tall grass).

Can't go over it. (Can't go over it).

Can't go under it. (Can't go under it).

Can't go around it. (Can't go around it).

Have to go through it. (Have to go through it)."

They'd follow the actions and sounds the leader would make, pretending to go through tall grass. The same can be said about grief. There is no getting around it or away from it. The griever must go through it. Believing that grief will eventually go away if you avoid it is a myth. It simply won't happen. Pretending it doesn't exist or trying to isolate oneself from it only prolongs the grieving process. In order to get through grief, we must allow ourselves to grieve. We can't experience grief without feeling the pain of it. No one likes pain or wants to experience suffering of any kind, but the sad reality is that each of us will experience it at various times throughout our lives.

So what is grief? It's an emotional coping response that our body and brain undertake in processing the loss of someone or something dear to us. Grief is universal—everyone will experience it at some point. Yet, at the same time, it's deeply personal. It's a natural reaction to loss that's built into us by God's design. Grief is a process experienced by the grieving person, and the length of time that it lasts cannot be controlled by the griever. Some may grieve their loss for months or years. There is no set time frame, nor should one be imposed on the one who grieves. It's hard work trying to deal with grief. It's multi-faceted. Our grief is an expression of our love for the one we have lost, and a time limit cannot be predicted or expected.

There is a plethora of emotions that are part of grief. Your world is turned upside down. You experience a literal avalanche of feelings—many overlapping each other simultaneously. Shock, denial, fear, confusion, and incredible sadness hit you like a tidal wave. Then there's anxiety, worry, and a depth of loneliness you've never known before. You feel disoriented, and there's a deep hopelessness as you wonder how you'll survive all of this. The emptiness and physical pain make you wonder if you're going to have a heart attack or stroke. In extreme cases, if you're struggling with depression, contemplating suicide or are using drugs or alcohol to dull your pain, please consider getting professional help right away.

Some believe they can avoid grief by staying busy, but this isn't true. We must allow ourselves to experience the feelings of pain and sadness, along with the other emotions that attach themselves to grief and loss. Our grief is birthed out of our love for that person. Grieving is a means of honouring our loved one's memory. Don't deny yourself the time to grieve, and don't try to rush the process. Grief cannot be rushed and it doesn't punch a time clock. It is through experiencing grief that healing comes.

I questioned where grief came from. How did it come into existence? Who was the first one to experience grief? When God created the world, grief didn't exist. Genesis 1 and 2 describe how God said everything He created was very good. There was no sadness, no pain, no confusion, no sin. He created the world and man out of love and a desire to be in relationship with His creation. So where did grief come from? Genesis chapters 3-6 describe how sin entered the world. The relationship God so desired was now broken, and sin became rampant. The first record we have of grief is found in Genesis 6:6 (NKJV), where we're told that because of man's sin, "... *He [God] was grieved in His heart."* God was the first One to experience grief. This wasn't how God had designed the world to be. Man was given a free will to choose between good and evil, and through deception, man chose to believe evil and this broke God's heart. He grieved the loss of the ones with whom He wanted to have a relationship. God created man out of love, but His love was rejected, and it grieved His heart. He felt the pain of His loss. Grief was born out of God's love for His creation... for mankind. Similarly, my grief over the loss of Ron was born out of my love for him. We don't grieve over that which we don't love.

One evening as I got off the elevator, I met my next-door neighbour. We exchanged greetings and then he asked the question, *"So, have you moved on?"* Are you kidding? Did I hear you just ask if I've *moved on?* I'm still trying to figure out if this is just a bad dream! I still wasn't over the shock of it. My life felt like it had crashed and burned. I had lost the most important person in my life. We built a life together and now it has been brutally snatched away from us. We will never experience that relationship again. *"NO!"* I responded. It had only been three months. Did he really think I should be moving on? It felt like Ron's life no longer mattered to him and I was offended. Everything I said was met with the words, *"I know."* Yet, how could he possibly know what I'm feeling and what I'm going through? He's not me! I finally couldn't take it anymore and said, *"With all due respect, you don't know. You're about to walk into your condo and be met by your wife. I am about to walk into mine and be met with loneliness and silence."* I think at that point he maybe had a small inkling of what grief might be like for a griever. As author Clarissa Moll says, *"Moving on is… not what you do when you leave a grave."*[5]

The very first response of grief that I experienced was shock. My family witnessed it and to this day, I have no memory of what took place. I couldn't remember my phone code to call my daughters to let them know about their dad. I don't recall speaking

---

5. Clarissa Moll, *Beyond the Darkness:* Carol Stream, IL: Tyndale House Publishers, 2002, 162.

with them. I don't recall going in to see Ron. I don't remember the ride home and how I kept asking the same questions. When I told my sister that I was praying God would give me back my memory, her response was, *"I'm praying He won't."*

It took me four months to get over the shock and to face the harsh reality that Ron was never coming home to me. Getting over the shock doesn't equal getting over grief. Shock can actually pause our body and brain's ability to work through the myriad of emotions that bombard us, but also the new reality we have been forced to live. I was trying to navigate my life in a fog.

Denial goes hand in hand with shock. I simply couldn't come to terms with the fact that Ron was gone and my life had taken a dramatic turn that I wasn't prepared for. I'd walk out to the living room expecting to see him sitting in his chair reading. I'd catch myself wanting to ask him what he wanted for dinner. He always took the recycling down to the recycling room and one time I caught myself preparing to ask him to take it down. Denial is a defensive response that causes us to refuse to believe or accept something that creates pain or anxiety—like the unexpected death of someone we love. It's a natural part of the grieving process that gives us time to process and accept the information we've received.

Five months into losing Ron, I received an invitation to have coffee with a lady who knew my parents years ago. Another lady was invited, so we drove together. During the course of the visit, the hostess said she hadn't seen me at church for a number of weeks and started emphasizing that I needed to be there. On top of that, she added that I needed to be involved in the ministry of the church. At that point I asked if she knew what happened. She didn't. So, I told her. She had no concept of what Ron went through nor the shock my body went into upon losing him. We had just started attending the church four months before Ron died. We didn't know many people at all. We were planning to get involved but hadn't decided yet where we would serve. As I got into the car with the other lady who came with me that day, I just looked at her and said, *"Why do I feel like I am being made out to be a backslider?"*

    I felt like a sense of guilt had been imposed on me. I explained that I don't just jump into the first ministry someone suggests I get involved in. I've never approached ministry that way. I couldn't bear coming and sitting by myself in a church where I didn't know many people. I didn't want to make a spectacle of myself when I felt so emotionally raw. I wasn't able to hold back the tears when unexpected waves and triggers overwhelmed me. It made me wonder why people feel they have the right to make such decisions on my behalf. It was another confirmation to me that there's a need to learn how to talk to and support those who are grieving deeply.

    When a person we dearly love dies, we don't stop loving them. A spouse, a child, a parent, or anyone we've been exceptionally close to. We don't bury our love for them when we bury them. They live on in our hearts, minds, and memories. They're a part of who we are and always will be. We think of them 24/7 when they're gone. We think of what we had with them, and what we don't have now. They're our first thought when we wake up and our last thought when we go to bed. They're with us throughout the day.

As I'm writing this book, I see an elderly couple from the condo building across the road out walking every day. He will take her hand, or she will slip her arm through his, and they continue on their walk together. And every time I see them, I thank God—with tears streaming down my face—that they have each other. I pray for them, asking God to give them a few more years together. I now know the pain of not being able to walk with Ron and have him take my hand or me slipping my arm through the crook of his. I don't wish that on anyone. There simply isn't any pain like the pain of losing someone you love with all your heart. Just as we can't stop the waves from pounding the seashore, so it is with the waves of grief and sadness that flood our souls.

You've probably heard the comparison between grief and an amputation. Grief is a lot like an amputation. It isn't the same as if you sprained your wrist or broke your ankle because those can be fixed and can heal so you can be as good as new in time. However, an amputation means something has been cut off, never to return. You don't really 'recover' from an amputation. You have to make adjustments to your new lifestyle, and it can be very painful physically, emotionally, and mentally.

    I learned about some of the necessary adjustments from my aunt. Aunt Lois was a very funny woman. She loved to play practical jokes on her family. My children and I nicknamed her "Great Aunt Lois"—not only because she was their great aunt, but because she was pretty great in other ways. There was a period of time, however, when the practical jokes stopped. Life seemed to have taken a dramatic turn for her. She ended up having her leg amputated above the knee. I learned some significant things about amputation because of her. I never knew there was such a thing as phantom pain. She would feel pain in her leg... except her leg was no longer there. How could that be? There were also major adjustments that needed to be made to accommodate her ability to recover—getting a prosthetic leg that fit properly, physiotherapy in learning how to walk with it, learning how to care for it, as well as the stump of her leg. It is a lengthy recovery process, and it was something she had to endure for the remainder of her life. One of the biggest adjustments, however, was when her son told her she couldn't continue living alone in her home. It was too much to maintain, and he was concerned for her safety because of all the stairs. She ended up moving into a retirement home. This became an additional loss with which she had to live.

Grief is like an amputation. Someone has been cut off from your life and cannot return. They are gone, and you're left trying to figure out how your new life will continue without them. The pain is deep and unpredictable. It has become your new normal, and you despise it.

There are times during grief that we literally have to remind ourselves to breathe, especially at the onset of it. It's unrelenting and profoundly sad. It's all-consuming and inexplicably overwhelming at the same time. It's being on an emotional rollercoaster that never stops. You feel like your heart has been ripped out of your chest. The loneliness is beyond words, and you wonder if you'll ever stop crying. You keep hoping it's a bad dream that you'll wake up from, but you gradually realize that it's your new reality, and you hate it.

And it leaves me asking, "How can grief possibly be a *gift?*"

The Gift of Grief

Chapter Three

Are There Really Five Stages to Grief?

We were created for relationship not only in life, but in death as well.
We were never created to grieve alone.

I was having dinner with Jeanne and Jim one evening when Jim started talking about how death was very much a part of family and community life at the turn of the 20th Century. Back in those days, people who were dying weren't sent to long-term care facilities or hospitals to die. Long-term care facilities as we know them today didn't even exist at that time. Instead, the loved one died at home, surrounded by their family who were with them through the process of their dying and death. At the turn of the 20th Century, there were only a handful of funeral homes in Canada, so the body of the deceased was usually kept in the family home, and people from the community would come to visit the family and pay their respects. This was followed by a church service and an interment at the local cemetery, where friends and family would say their final goodbyes to the deceased.

The average life expectancy in Canada in 1900 was 50 years or less. Some lived longer and others succumbed much earlier. The infant mortality rate was high in those days due to a lack of medications and knowledgeable medical care. Influenza, bronchitis, tuberculosis, pneumonia, heart disease, stroke, cancer, polio, and diabetes were all major contributors to death rates at the turn of the century. Medical care was not what it is today.

Breakthroughs in medicine have greatly increased life expectancy. For instance, Banting and Best discovered insulin in 1921. Alexander Fleming's discovery of penicillin in 1928 was the first antibiotic for killing bacterial infections. Selman Waksman was awarded the Nobel Prize in Physiology or Medicine in 1952 for his discovery of streptomycin, the first effective antibiotic for tuberculosis. In 1955, an American named Jonas Salk developed the vaccine that would eradicate polio. All of these and other medical discoveries contributed to a major increase in life expectancy. Today, the pharmaceutical industry is a multi-billion-dollar enterprise. Science and technology have contributed to the advancements that have led to longer life spans over the past 100 years. Along with the advancement of medical science came better hygiene regulations and improved nutritional standards, leading to lifestyle changes that contributed to our longevity and outlook on life.

As life expectancy dramatically increased, the way of trying to cope with the terminally ill and death also changed. Society became more uncomfortable with the reality and inconvenience of death and dying. The focus on living one's final days at home began to switch to spending their final days in hospitals and government-run facilities. Gradually, society became more removed from being 'hands-on' in the care of their loved one in their last days. In a sense, the medical professionals became more of the primary caregivers because those who were dying were hospitalized under their care. Whether we realized it or not, it contributed to our removing ourselves from being intimately involved in the process of death and dying. It also contributed to our drawing away from having these conversations. It became more conducive for us to allow the staff in hospitals and long-term care facilities to attend to our loved ones, thereby giving us the choice of how involved we would be. Isn't it interesting that the more we learn about death and dying, the more uncomfortable we have become talking about it? We want to avoid it and don't want to think about it.

In 1969, the world-renowned Swiss-American psychiatrist, Elizabeth Kubler-Ross, published her groundbreaking and internationally recognized book entitled *On Death and Dying*. In it she presented her findings based on 200 conversations she documented with terminally ill patients. These patients were living with life-threatening conditions and diseases ranging from COPD to HIV. In having these conversations, Kubler-Ross noticed there were similarities among these terminally ill patients. Their responses seemed to follow a pattern or stages of grieving as their diseases progressed which she referred to as the five stages of grief. The majority of patients tended to follow a certain order as they came to terms with their illness:

denial, anger, bargaining, depression, and acceptance.

It's important to put Kubler-Ross's work into the context of when she wrote her book. It was an era when people were feeling more and more self-sufficient, but also becoming more introspective. During that era, psychiatry as we know it was in its infancy and no research was being done in this area. At the onset, she was met with resistance from the medical community. Her real purpose in conducting these conversations with those who were dying was to build dignity and respect for them. It was her hope that the community at large wouldn't view them as cast-offs, but as people who could impact those around them with their personal stories of dying. Her goal was to give the dying a voice and open the door for people to have conversations about death.

It was Kubler-Ross who initiated the idea of hospice and palliative care for the dying and terminally ill. Over the decades, her efforts gradually resulted in improvements in the mental health field for millions. Her book became the trailblazer in psychiatry for others to build on.

Somewhere along the line, the five stages of grief that terminally ill patients may experience began to be imposed on all kinds of grief, including those who are bereaved. Unfortunately, this misunderstanding that 'everyone' will go through the five stages is still very much a part of our present society's thinking. It has raised questions and confusion for many because they don't see their grief over the loss of a loved one fitting into that pattern—but it was never intended to because grief doesn't follow a straight path.

No two people will grieve the same. We may experience similar journeys in some ways, but our grieving is unique to each of us because we're uniquely different from every other person. How we grieve has many influencing factors—cultural and religious beliefs, our family upbringing and interactions, our personality, and our relationship to the one who died. The one thing we do have in common is that grief is inevitable when we experience the pain and suffering of losing someone very dear to us. How we navigate through grief reflects the heart, mind, and soul of each individual. Grief travels at the speed of the one grieving. It isn't a prescribed sequence of steps to be followed. That's why a time frame can't be applied to it. We simply can't prepare ahead of time for how we'll react when we lose someone we love. Each person grieves in their own way, in their own time. To place limitations or expectations on them is to actually set them back.

There's so much to learn about grief and loss. We need to realize that grief is not a problem to be solved, it's a journey to be walked. The goal is never to get over grief. The truth is, we'll always carry the grief of losing someone so precious to us because they're, in fact, a part of us. We need to learn how to walk forward amid our grief.

The Gift of Grief

Chapter Four

How do You Grieve?

Fear not, for I am with you; Be not dismayed,
for I am your God.
I will strengthen you, Yes, I will help you,
I will uphold you with My righteous right hand.[6]

In 1983 we received the heartbreaking news that my cousin had died by suicide. He walked into the bay and never walked out again. It was such a shock to all of us. In high school, he was the top of his class. Unfortunately, he was bullied by some students because he was very quiet and reserved. He was only 21 years old and had just gotten engaged. We all thought life was looking good for him, but he was fighting the demons of depression. Little did we know that he was struggling so deeply that he'd end his life.

His mom grieved openly and went for professional counselling to deal with her grief. His dad took a different approach, unfortu-

---

6. Isaiah 41:10 NKJV.

nately. He refused to talk about his son. It was as if he never existed. My sister and I had made a family video for our parents that year, and Mom wanted the rest of the family to see it. When the picture of my cousin appeared, my uncle immediately got up and walked out of the room. He refused to watch the rest of the video. My mom wanted to go after him, but my aunt shook her head and told her it wouldn't do any good. He would refuse to talk about it.

It reminded me of how someone will take a pair of scissors and cut a person out of a picture when they've had a falling out with them. They don't want to be reminded of them. This was what it was like with my uncle. His son was removed from his life, never to be talked about again. Was it a matter of my uncle not loving his son? No, not at all. My uncle tended to be very strict and his firstborn bore the brunt of that. He refused to go to counselling in spite of how much my aunt tried to convince him to go with her. My aunt dealt with her grief through tears and talking about her son. My uncle, however, lived with unresolved grief for the rest of his life.

How a person grieves is unique to them. Just as people show love in different ways, they also express grief in different ways. It's true that men and women grieve differently, but it doesn't mean that all men grieve one way and all women grieve another. A husband will grieve differently than his wife. Siblings grieve differently than each other. One may be very emotional, while another keeps their emotions in check and looks for a different outlet to deal with their grief. There's no 'one-size-fits-all' when going through loss. Some men may follow the more feminine description of grieving, and some women may follow the more masculine description. It's important to recognize that there's no right or wrong way to grieve or communicate our grief to others.

Throughout our lives, our thought processes have been continually influenced by relationships we've had in the past, be it through family and friends, during our school years, or throughout our careers. Many of us have grown up in a society that taught *"big boys don't cry."* Men crying has been misconstrued as a sign of weakness and vulnerability. They're supposed to have a tougher exterior and to suppress their emotions. It was instilled in many men that they're to be the rock of the family at all times when everyone else is in a state of emotional shock and upheaval. They believe the false expectation that they're always to be in control. Whether they recognize it or not, they're unconsciously relaying the same message to their children.

We know that men and women are biologically different. However, we may not be aware that they're different neurologically. Dr. Michael Shapiro, Director of Behavioural Medicine at Duke Medical School's Southern Regional Area Health Center in North Carolina writes: *"It is a proven fact that there are actually differences in the structure and chemistry of male vs. female brains. These differences begin in utero, before we're even born!"* He goes on to say that during childhood development is when a girl's brain starts to process information in different ways than a boy's brain. Females have what's referred to as 'verbal centres' on both sides of the brain, whereas males only have one verbal centre on the left side. Dr. Shapiro continues, *"Females often have a larger hippocampus (the "centre" of human memory) with a higher density of neural connections in that area. As a result, females take in and absorb more sensory and emotional information than their male counterparts. It has also been shown that male brains use more grey matter (information and action-centred areas of the brain) when processing information, while females use more white matter (which governs "higher order" reasoning and thinking). This is why females tend to be better at multi-tasking, are usually better at interpreting emotions and seem to have 'women's intuition'."*[7]

I recall being invited back to someone's home after a funeral. It was interesting to observe the relationship dynamic that unfolded with regard to men and women. The women sat in the living room, talking and reminiscing about the deceased loved one, while the men were downstairs in the rec room, which was like a giant playroom complete with a pinball machine and various game tables. The women engaged in talking with each other. The men engaged in activities. Dr. Shapiro's explanation sheds light on why men often ask women to just give the highlights of a

---

7. Michael Shapiro, *The Difference Between Men and Women: Is It All in the Brain?*, accessed February 5, 2025, https://www.southernregionalahec.org/men-women-brain/

conversation rather than share every single detail. It also explains why women, when talking to a man, often want their undivided attention with no outside distractions.

Women tend to be more relational than men. Just walk into a hair salon. Women talk about everything from family and children to work and personal relationships. Women bond with each other more quickly. They invite each other into their homes for coffee, to go out for lunch, and to go shopping together. They take their kids to the park together. In a church setting, women are readily involved in Bible studies, small groups, support groups, moms with tots groups, and evening events focused on missions and outreach ministries to women in the community. Women communicate with each other emotionally.

Men communicate, but generally not about emotional issues. They talk more about work, sports, travel, and family in more general terms. They tend to lock their emotions inside. Many men find it difficult to even share their deep emotions with their wives. Oftentimes, they don't know how to communicate their grief in words so they remain silent, trying to deal with their pain internally.

It's crucial for women to understand that they shouldn't make assumptions about how the men in their lives communicate their grief. Some men will cry, but there are many who won't. Because women are emotionally wired, it's easy to misinterpret a man's lack of tears as not caring or not grieving their loss. It's important to understand that a lack of tears doesn't equal a lack of grief. It could be that the men in their lives may be expressing their tears and sadness when they're alone.

Both men and women experience grief and feel the pain of loss. Women need to be supportive of men through their grieving process. For those men who try to stifle their grief, they need to recognize that trying to avoid the pain of grief isn't actually dealing with it and won't make it go away. Men need the reinforcement of knowing that the emotions they feel are an expression of their love for their loved one. It's crucial that men and women grieve in the way that's most comfortable to them.

No matter how a person grieves, however, it's important that they understand that they don't have to travel this road alone. They were never intended to go through grief in isolation, and if they don't have a support system in place with family and friends, there's support available through various grief support groups, professional counsellors, and social workers.

Part Two

GRIEF

The Thief

The Gift of Grief

Chapter Five

Lest We Forget

*For He Himself has said,
"I will never leave you nor forsake you."*[8]

One day in April, I noticed the City of Barrie had put up the Remembrance Day flags. Each flag bears the face and name of a Canadian who fought for our freedom and died during WWI and WWII. I was surprised because these flags usually go up in time for November 11th—Remembrance Day. This was over six months ahead of schedule, and then I was reminded that it was the anniversary of Vimy Ridge and the flags had been put up to remind us of Canada's role.

On the top of each flag are the words, *"Lest We Forget."* These flags are a reminder that our freedom, as a country, was because of the men and women who fought in those wars. They don't deserve to be forgotten with their pictures in photo albums

---

8. Hebrews 13:5   NKJV.

packed away in boxes and stored on dusty shelves. They have faces. They have names. They have families they loved and who loved them. Their families were left heartbroken when they learned that they didn't survive the horrors of war. How they must have grieved! It touched my heart deeply.

One of the things many grieving people say they fear the most is that they'll eventually forget their loved ones. They fear they'll forget the sound of their voice, their touch, the special memories they shared together, that special look in their eyes. It's another aspect of grief to deal with and it can leave the grieving one overwhelmed with guilt and sadness. Unjustified feelings can feel justified. We believe that if we can't remember their voice, their laugh, or any other special trait, we're being disloyal and are betraying their memory. *How could I not remember this about them? If they knew this, would they think I don't love them anymore? They'd be so hurt!* We can truly feel like we're being ambushed by grief. When we first experience the loss of a loved one, grief automatically puts our mind on rewind. We play everything over and over again, not wanting to forget the details. We're consumed by the shock of what's happened to them. It's our way of holding our loved ones near to us.

I believe there are two reasons why we may have a fear of forgetting our loved ones. First, we may believe that if we forget something about them, we've started to *move on*—that we're *letting go* of them and are *leaving them behind*. That can be a definite sign of betrayal in our minds. Second, we can impose an unbearable guilt on ourselves for not remembering every detail of their life and our time together. Guilt is very hard to reconcile during grief. Part of the journey of grief, however, is coming to terms with the reality that our loved one is gone. It's also recognizing our need to begin moving forward in our healing.

I thought a lot about those words *"to move on."* When we hear those words, we associate the following meanings: to abandon; to leave behind; to put aside. I have no intention of *moving on*. You don't just throw away a lifetime of memories you made with that person. You don't just set aside a 41-year marriage and move on. But what I need to do to bring healing in my life is *move forward*. The intention of these words is different. They suggest: to continue to make progress; to build upon the past; to move forward. *"Getting over a loss is moving on as if the loss never happened—shutting the door behind you and doing your best to pretend the pain away. Getting 'through' a loss, however, is reaching a place where you accept the horrible events that brought so much grief and sorrow, while finding the strength through God's grace to continue forward in life despite the loss."*[9] The Apostle Paul says in Philippians 3:14 (NASB), *"I press on toward the goal for the prize of the upward call of God in Christ Jesus."* It promotes the idea of continuing to move forward, completing the journey I've already started. The same

---

9. Bill Prater, *How to Get Through What You'll Never Get Over*: Lancaster, CA: Striving Together Publications, 2022, p.18.

can be applied to my journey with grief. I press on—I'm moving forward to complete the journey I've already started.

When we're thrown into grief, our thinking automatically reverts to the past. We think of what we had. We focus on what we've lost. This is normal, but as our journey progresses, we have to make decisions about the present and the future. It doesn't mean we've forgotten the past. We carry it in our hearts with us as we move forward.

I'm grateful I live in the age of technology. I have a video of Ron on my phone, and I'm so grateful for it because I not only see and hear him moving and speaking—he is *alive* in it. For 49 brief seconds as I watch it, I feel he's alive with me at that moment. Videos, taped messages, a voicemail, old family movies that might have captured our loved one's voice and movements are all a source of calm in the midst of the storm that otherwise rages in us. For that, I'm truly grateful.

I have totes full of pictures of us from over the years—of our family and friends, our wedding and honeymoon, the trips we took, special outings and get-togethers, birthdays and anniversaries, and holiday celebrations like Christmas and Thanksgiving. There are hospital pictures from when our daughters were born and pictures from when they got married. Each one is a treasure that holds special recollections of the wonderful days we shared. I treasure that last picture of Brittany with her dad in the hospital before she left to go to Halifax. These photos don't have any monetary value, but they're priceless to us. They're a source of healing in our journey with grief.

While visiting with my daughter, Shauna, and her family in Nova Scotia after Ron died, I asked her what she missed the most about her dad. She said it was his presence and his sense of humour. Ron was known for his corny jokes. He could be loud, especially at family gatherings or when watching his beloved Maple Leafs or Blue Jays. He was an extrovert—definitely a people person. He was the eighth of ten children, so he learned at an early age how to make himself heard. He also loved to participate in a good debate or discussion. He could always get a conversation started and keep it going. For Brittany, it was his hugs, his jokes, and his compassion for people. It was never beneath him to help someone in need. For me it was a number of things—his presence, his laugh, his hugs and kisses, taking my hand, and his constant reminder for me to ask him for help when lifting heavy things. I loved the way he'd say my name and that special look in his eyes that only I was the recipient of. But one of the things I miss the most is hearing him pray. He'd often complete his prayers with the words, *"...in the strong Name of Jesus."* He respected the sovereignty of God. I loved our discussions about God's Word and the numerous discussions we had over the years with my parents around their kitchen table.

A few months after Ron's passing, I met Bill Prater, a pastor from Kansas who was a guest speaker at a church I visited. The topic of his message was grief. He wrote a little book entitled, *How To Get Through What You'll Never Get Over*. The title says it all. His 35-year-old son was killed in a freak accident. He was working on his truck and it fell on him. He was killed instantly. In the account of his son, Bill said, *"The loss of TJ is one Katie and I will never get over. And honestly, I don't want to. TJ was too important to me to pretend that life just goes on the same with or without him... We don't look at people who are experiencing life's joys and tell them to just get over it. So why should we assume people should just get over life's sorrows?"*[10]

We'll always have a special bond with our departed loved ones. Though we grieve their absence with us physically, they continue to live in our hearts and minds. We need to give ourselves grace.

Be kind to yourself and give yourself the time and space to grieve and heal as you move forward. Though we may forget some things over the course of time, the one thing—the most important thing—is that we won't forget the love we shared.

---

10. Bill Prater, *How to Get Through What You'll Never Get Over*: Lancaster, CA: Striving Together Publications, 2022, p.9,15.

The Gift of Grief

Chapter Six

Good and Bad Anger

... casting all your anxiety upon Him, because He cares for you.[11]

When I was five years old, my mother and I were in the car on our way to the store. As she was parking the car, my mother's high school principal saw her and came over to the car to say hello. In the course of the conversation, he said, *"And this must be your little girl."* Smiling, and with a heart full of pride, my mother responded, *"Yes, this is Marcia."* My response was obviously based on something that had transpired between my mother and me before meeting the principal. I don't recall what it was, but with daggers in my eyes, I looked at my mother and said, *"I hate you!"* I have no recollection of the principal's reaction, but I'm sure he probably said a hasty goodbye so my mother could deal with me. My mother was completely humiliated, as you can well imagine. I don't recall us going into the store; however, I do recall

---

11. I Peter 5:7   NASB.

the ride back to my grandmother's house, where we were visiting for the weekend. I knew I was in big trouble. As my mother took my hand upon entering my grandmother's house, I vividly remember saying, *"I'm sorry, Mommy. I didn't mean it! I'm sorry! I didn't mean it!"* That was a spanking I've never forgotten! Years later, as we laughed at this story, my grandmother said she figured I must've done something really bad and knew to stay out of it. I wish I could recall what the issue was, but it was obviously something that really irritated me, and I wasn't afraid to let my mother know what I thought of her at that moment.

What is anger? It's an emotion that's characterized by displeasure or antagonism toward a situation or a person that you feel has wronged you in some way. It can be brought on in a number of ways. It could be the result of a betrayal or some form of injustice. It could be the result of an injury, cruel actions or words. It could be brought on by jealousy, disappointment, or discrimination. There's a wide variety of things that can trigger anger. The intensity of anger can range from indignation to rage. It can be displayed through aggression or by retaliating against something or someone. It usually wants some form of justification or retribution.

So what's the *root cause* of anger? Anger is often referred to as a secondary emotion, meaning some other underlying emotion has brought on anger. I recall seeing a picture of an iceberg, where the small portion above the water's surface represented anger.

Beneath the surface was a much larger mass, which represented the primary emotions that often trigger the anger response. The underlying root of most people's anger is a sense of powerlessness, as there's a feeling of being unable to control the circumstances. Anger can be triggered by a wide range of emotions—frustration, resentment, humiliation, and impatience. It can be brought on by sadness, stress, rejection, or feeling threatened. It can also stem from fear or past trauma. Often, anger piggybacks on these and other emotions, which can create feelings of vulnerability or disappointment that can quickly converge into anger.

Anger can arise when someone treats us in such a way that has negative repercussions. Perhaps you grew up in a home environment that negatively impacted your childhood. Perhaps you endured a painful separation or divorce that left your life feeling irreparably shattered. Or maybe you have a child living with a debilitating disease that will shorten their life expectancy, robbing them of the joys that healthy children get to experience daily. Naturally, you might feel angry that your child hasn't been dealt a fair hand in this life. It's not uncommon for someone to feel extreme anger over the loss of someone who was dearly loved. Anger can be a natural response to both physical and emotional pain. Anger is always preceded by feelings of pain or discomfort about a situation or person. In some cases, anger can be a means of trying to regain the power and control that was lost.

When I asked others how they'd define anger, many described it as *'a negative emotion,' 'a bad mood,' 'a response to something unkind that was done or said to them or a loved one,' 'being confrontational,' 'someone being out of control,' or 'accusatory.'* These definitions may conjure up pictures in our minds of people yelling, turning red in the face, possibly swearing, or reaching their boiling point. Extreme anger in others can evoke feelings of fear in us, especially if there's a lack of self-control. Ultimately, anger is always directed at someone or something.

However, there are some who choose to suppress their anger. The problem with suppressing anger is that it could eventually erupt like a volcano, spewing the lava of their wrath on everybody and everything around them. It can have a damaging effect on everyone. There's no gratification in unresolved anger because it's waiting to be dealt with and can't go away on its own. The worst part about suppressing anger is how it can alienate people from others and from God. Suppressed anger can also lead to health concerns such as high blood pressure and heart issues. On top of health issues, it can also cause relational issues with family and friends, as well as work productivity. It can lead to social isolation, bitterness, and possible depression for some if they allow their anger to go unaddressed.

For the griever, unresolved anger concerning their loved one's death is unresolved grief. To suppress anger is to delay facing it and coming to terms with it. It prevents one from moving forward. One young man I spoke with said he recognized that he has unresolved anger over the death of two close family members who died over the course of a number of years. He said he believed that if he pushed it down and ignored it, it would eventually go away, and he would be able to move on. He now sees that's not the case and acknowledges that he needs to deal with it. God invites us to come to Him with our broken hearts, our shattered dreams and our unresolved anger. He wants us to give them all to Him, trusting that He will bring beauty out of the ashes of our pain, loss, and suffering.

The Bible is full of examples of people who were angry. Angry at their brother. Angry at a parent. Angry at a friend. Angry at God. Cain's anger toward his brother, Abel, was born out of jealousy. It was so intense that he killed his brother. Ultimately, his anger was toward God for rejecting his sacrifice.[12]

The book of Esther in the Bible tells the inspiring, true story of Queen Esther. In it, an evil man named Haman went into a rage because Mordecai, a Jewish man, refused to bow down to him. Haman hated the Jewish people. When Mordecai refused to bow down to him, Haman's anger spurred him on to devise a plan to annihilate all the Jewish people. It's an amazing story of how God led a young Jewish woman named Hadassah (Esther), to become a queen for the purpose of saving her people from annihilation at the hands of an evil, hateful man. In the end, Haman, the rage-filled villain, was the one put to death.

It's not uncommon to experience anger when you lose a loved

---

12. See Genesis 4:3-16

one. It's a normal response for many as they walk their journey of grief. When you feel anger toward the person who died, it's often because you feel their death could've been prevented. Perhaps their death or loss of health was due to a poor choice or unwise decision on their part. Maybe it was a family member or friend who didn't take good care of themselves. Perhaps it was related to alcohol or drug abuse. Maybe it was because they didn't follow through on advice given to them by a doctor or medical professional. It could be any number of things. Perhaps you feel anger toward them because their death has negatively impacted your life in more ways than one. You might feel abandoned by them, especially if you didn't get to say goodbye to them the way you wanted. There may have been things that were learned after the fact, which have now complicated how to handle the situation. You're angry at how it's left you feeling empty inside and alone. You may also feel robbed of the time you could've had with that person.

I've had friends share that they don't blame their loved one, but have seething anger toward their healthcare provider who oversaw their loved one's care and treatment. It left them with a million questions, intense bitterness, and resentment. Perhaps they gave a wrong diagnosis. Maybe the doctor didn't seek a second opinion as requested by the family. Or, it may be that an incorrect treatment was prescribed. It isn't the first time people have felt they knew better than the medical professionals.

Years ago, my uncle had leukemia, and my aunt took him to the hospital to have another blood transfusion. She commented to the nurse that the blood in the bag looked *"sludgy."* The nurse said it was fine, but my aunt challenged her. The nurse again said reassuringly that it was fine. By the time my aunt was driving my uncle home, he started to feel unwell. Usually, after a blood transfusion, his energy level would increase; but when they arrived at their home, he collapsed on the driveway. He was taken back to the hospital, but within a couple of days, he was gone. A year later, the local paper headlined an article about the hospital having 'bad blood.' My aunt was adamant it was the same time she had taken her husband for the blood transfusion. She was furious and wanted accountability. She wanted retribution. Her son said there was no point because the blood transfusion bags were long gone, and she would have no way of proving it was the cause of my uncle's death. She had to let it go, but that wasn't something she could do right away. She needed to work through her anger.

Then, there's self-inflicted anger. *I should have… I could have… but I didn't.* Self-inflicted anger and pain are very hard to deal with. We can be angry at ourselves because we couldn't control what happened. We can question whether we could've prevented it or at the very least, changed the outcome for them. At the onset of grief, we don't have answers, and quite honestly, we aren't ready to receive them. We're in such a state of sadness, and for many, shock. Death never consulted with us. We had no say in whether they should live or die. We had no say about how we needed more time with them. **We had no say!** It can leave us feeling completely out of control. It's like being suspended in mid-air, having no way to come down. As time moves forward, these feelings can begin to dominate our thinking, and the anger begins to show itself. We can blame ourselves for not being more proactive.

It's not unusual for some to be angry at God and perhaps blame Him for what happened to their loved one. The 'why' questions start to arise in their hearts. They may question why God didn't do anything. He knew this was going to happen—why didn't He do something to stop it? Why didn't He give them more time? Why didn't He respond the way they wanted? Why did He allow this to happen?

It's very hard to have perspective amid our sorrow and grief. If we'd only give God the opportunity to tell us His perspective on death, we might have a clearer understanding of how He hates death as much as we do.

Perhaps what we really need is to see what God says about death. Here's what He says:

- We weren't created to live a life followed by death. Death didn't exist when He created the world (Genesis 1-3).

- Because mankind's sin ushered in the curse/penalty of death, every person will experience death since none of us has lived a sinless life (Genesis 3:17-19).

- He said that there's an appointed time for everything in this life. The words 'appointed time' imply something that's been previously arranged or established ahead of time. King Solomon said that includes a time to be born and a time to die (Ecclesiastes 3:1-2).

- God created a 'God-void' in our hearts that only He can fill. We were created to live with Him eternally. He has set eternity in our hearts. Although sin has separated us from God, there's nothing and no one that can complete and satisfy that 'eternity void' apart from Him (Ecclesiastes 3:11).

- God took on flesh and blood in the form of Jesus so that He could identify with mankind and take our place in destroying the power of death's hold on us (Hebrews 2:14).

- Jesus willingly went to the cross alone and suffered pain and death beyond our wildest imagination so we wouldn't have to suffer our pain alone (Isaiah 53).

- Death hasn't won the final war. Since Jesus rose to life on the third day, He defeated death (I Corinthians 15:55-56).

- God's Word tells us just as through one man (Adam) sin entered the world, and death entered through sin, causing death to spread to all of mankind; so by one man's obedience (Jesus) many are made righteous. (Romans 5:12,19)

- God takes no pleasure in seeing people die eternally when they refuse to receive His gift of forgiveness and salvation (Ezekiel 18:23).

- God did say that in this world we would experience trouble and affliction (John 16:33).

- He said if we would believe and place our faith in Him, we would not die eternally but would have everlasting life (John 3:16).

- Because Jesus rose to life on the third day, He overcame sin and the grave. He has gone to prepare a place for us and will return to receive us and take us there (John 14:2-3).

- God promises that for those who've put their faith in Christ, there will be no more death, tears, mourning, or crying in Heaven. (Revelation 21:4).

When I understand what He is promising me, I see a God who loves me so deeply. He wants to be reunited with me and all that's required of me is to receive by faith His gift of love, forgiveness, and salvation. He's created me to have a conscience and to recognize right from wrong. I see a God who doesn't treat me like a puppet, but gives me the free will to believe what He says is true or to reject Him. He gives me the freedom to tell Him I'm mad at Him about my loved one's death. He understands. He gets it because He's mad at death, too. He's given me the gift of His undeserved grace. I read how He's so moved by the sorrow of my heart, that He keeps my tears in a bottle (Psalm 56:8). I see a God who looks forward to reuniting me with my loved ones some day, never to be separated again (I Thessalonians 4:13-18). If He loves me this much, why would I choose to be angry with Him and blame Him for my loved one's death?

The issue isn't so much about the anger itself, but what we choose to do with it. Will we let it consume us? Will we let it ruin our relationships with others? With God? Or, will we allow it to teach us something? Are we willing to surrender our anger to His purposes? Our anger often leads to questioning others, but I believe it can be more helpful to truthfully ask and answer these questions of ourselves:

1) How does my anger make me feel?

When death invades our lives, our first response isn't anger. There's a sense of shock and sadness, even if we've been anticipating the death of our loved one due to a prolonged illness. Yes, we're relieved that they're no longer in pain and suffering, but we're acutely aware that their presence in our life is gone and it has a shock effect on us. They're gone. We feel the finality of their life, and it hurts beyond measure. We immediately feel powerless, and this precipitates a myriad of other emotions. Anger often rides on the back of emotions like sadness, loneliness, frustration, disappointment, distress, and regret, to name a few. As reality sets in, we begin to process what happened, how it happened and why it happened. We don't like it, we don't agree with it—be it right or wrong. We begin to feel the injustice of what death has taken from us and this, too, can cause us to feel anger. There's no gratification in this anger because it remains unresolved and leaves us with unanswered questions.

2) What or who is the focus of my anger?

Any number of situations and/or people can be the cause and focus of our anger. It's important to have an unbiased opinion, and grief simply doesn't afford us that luxury. If you or your family agree that something wasn't handled correctly, then you need to decide as a family what you feel would be the appropriate course of action.

In the case of blaming/holding our loved one responsible, we need to realize that our loved one may not have been able to deal with their own situation. For others, they may be dealing with the remorseful anger they carry because they believe their loved one's death may have been preventable. Someone is responsible, but who?

The reality is—and we all know this—all of us will die at an appointed time, short of when Jesus returns to take His own to Heaven. Would I be happy if God gave me 24 more hours with Ron? Yes and no. I would gladly take the extra 24 hours, but no matter what, I'd be right back where I was—wishing for more time and feeling like his life was taken far too soon for my liking.

Anger is not a sin. It's a natural response to a hurtful situation. It's how we choose to deal with it that's important. If our anger is used to deliberately seek revenge or cause harm to others, then it becomes a sin. Choosing to suppress anger or pretend it doesn't exist is avoiding the chance to deal with it constructively. Suppressing anger will never help us resolve it. It only delays facing it and coming to terms with it. It prevents us from moving forward.

The next three questions are personal. I'll leave them with you to answer on your own.

3) What will it take for me to forgive that person?

4) Am I willing to forgive them?

5) What will I do with my anger today?

The path to resolving anger is forgiveness. Blaming ourselves or someone else because we're angry will not bring healing. When left unresolved, it actually imprisons us. The more we believe that we or someone else is responsible for our loved one's death, the more difficult it becomes to forgive and let that go. We must come to the realization that some things will go unanswered, and there's nothing we can do to change that. What matters is what we do to help us move forward.

Personally, I didn't experience anger toward Ron, God, or the medical team who looked after him. When the surgeon came out to tell us how the first surgery went for Ron, he said it was successful. He said Ron's heart was good. Those words resonated with me. So, learning that he was gone after the second surgery didn't make any sense to me. Those words were a shock. For months after, I remember thinking, *"But the surgeon said his heart was good. How can this be?"* I could've very easily been angry with the surgeon, pronouncing guilt and blame on him for what went wrong, but there was one thing that prevented me from doing that—God's Word. He says:

"Thine eyes have seen my unformed substance;
And in Thy book they were all written,
The days that were ordained for me,
When as yet there was not one of them,"[13]

"Lord, make me to know my end,
And what is the measure of my days,
That I may know how frail I am.
Indeed, You have made my days as handbreadths,
And my age is as nothing before You;
Certainly every man at his best state is but vapor."[14]

"There is an appointed time for everything.
And there is a time for every event under Heaven -
A time to give birth, and a time to die;…"[15]

---

13. Psalm 139:16   NASB

14. Psalm 39:4-5   NKJV

15. Eccles. 3:1-2   NASB

The Bible compares our lives to a breath—a vapor. We're here today, gone tomorrow. To me, it didn't matter if Ron died on the operating table or was in a car accident. The days God had allotted to him were completed on November 25, 2023. It doesn't mean I like it. It doesn't mean I understand or agree with it, but it does mean that I recognize that our times are in His hands. It means there are things we simply have to accept by faith, trusting that His ways are higher than ours and that He has a purpose for everything that touches our lives. It means recognizing that because our knowledge is limited, we can't possibly grasp the eternal.

After Ron's funeral, I went through all kinds of journals and spiral notepads that he wrote in. For the most part a lot of it wasn't worth keeping. He even journaled when he opened a new toothbrush! I came across one note he wrote on a small, spiral notepad that I'll never part with. On it he wrote:

"Our time here is so fleeting. It is gone in the blink of an eye. (A dot compared to eternity). Words cannot express how my heart feels. Jesus has written my name in His scars. I am forever grateful. God was writing my story even before I was born. Thank you, Jesus!"

If you're overcome with anger about the death of your loved one, it might help to first examine the primary cause for your anger. Could it be fear? Is it a sense of powerlessness? Is it a result of deep sorrow? When you recognize what it is and begin to deal with it, surrender it to God. Release yourself from the right to judge. Just as He has forgiven you, so forgive others. Forgive yourself. Trust Him to redeem your pain. He can bring something good out of your pain if you'll let Him. One of the greatest gifts you can give yourself in the midst of your grief is the freedom that comes from forgiving and letting go of your anger.

The Gift of Grief

Chapter Seven

Regrets and Guilt; Forgiveness and Grace

For of His fulness we have all received, and grace upon grace.[16]

When I was seven years old, I had a friend, Melanie, who lived up the road from me. Her parents had a beautiful home with a big pool in the backyard. She invited me to go over to swim one summer afternoon. My mother wasn't home to ask, but I knew the rule was to stay on our property until she came home—but Melanie wanted me to come *now*. What should I do? I made an executive decision. I went. I had lots of fun, but I knew I needed to get home before my mother got back. So I ran home, took my wet bathing suit off and threw it under my bed so she wouldn't see it. I felt pretty proud of myself. I got to go swimming and my mother was none the wiser for it.

There was only one problem: I forgot all about the wet bathing suit under my bed. Oh, and did I mention that the floor

---

16. John 1:16 NASB.

was hardwood? I don't recall how many days it took before my mother found my bathing suit (the mildew smell probably led her to it). I do remember being confronted about it. Did I regret that I'd gone against my mother's instructions for me to stay on the property? No. Did I regret that I marked the hardwood floor where the bathing suit sat for days? No. Did I regret that I got caught? Ahhh—yes! Of course there was a punishment issued for disobedience. I wasn't allowed to go to Melanie's house for two weeks. The punishment said I was guilty, and I felt the guilt of that punishment.

Regret and guilt can be the result of a missed opportunity—something that should've been said or done, or similarly, something that should not have been said or done. Regret is often accompanied by great sadness and usually creates a feeling of guilt. Our guilt takes it one step further, invoking a feeling of blame and fault. It's an emotion that we often self-inflict upon ourselves, causing us to believe, right or wrong, that something negative or bad happened because of our response or lack thereof. At one time or another, everyone will have regrets and feel guilty about things they've said and done. It's part of life. For the griever, however, it's magnified when we lose someone we love dearly.

Feelings of regret and guilt are both part of the grieving process. Some of those situations may seem justified, but the vast majority aren't. There were things we intended to do or say, but never did. We can project our regrets into the future. We say things like, *"I could've done that, but I didn't." "Why didn't I say something when I had the opportunity?" "I should've known better."* The unfortunate thing about guilt and regret is that they don't visit us once and then leave. You think you've dealt with them, only to have them come back to replay and haunt you over and over again. This is where turning them over to the Lord is so important. He'll carry our grief and sorrows. We don't have to carry them alone.

 I regret that Ron never got to see or hold our first grandchild, Haddie. He gushed over the pictures and videos we'd get from our daughter. When we talked about going out East to meet her in October, Ron wanted to drive, but the rest of us said flying would make better use of our time together. Plus, he was still working so it meant he'd have to take additional time off work if we drove. It was obvious that he didn't want to fly for some reason, so he decided that he'd wait to meet her when they came for Christmas. I ended up flying to Halifax on my own. He never got to see or hold her. Sadly, he was gone a month before Christmas. When I look back in hindsight, I can't help but wonder if he was concerned about the impact flying would have on his heart, but he never gave any of us an indication that he wasn't feeling well. I had regrets that we didn't drive, as it would've given us more time together. After he died, I started to regret that I hadn't gone along with driving out East instead of flying on my own. If we'd driven out there, he would've seen and held her. I blame myself for this.

I regret that he never saw Shauna and Brandon's first home or visited their new church where they were putting down roots. He didn't get to see the golf course where Brandon was working. They had that in common with each other. Ron loved visiting golf courses. His first full-time job was in golf course construction. He always mentioned how he'd like to take Dave and Brandon to play a round of golf at Friday Harbour, where he worked. Good intentions, but the regret is that it never happened. He really wanted to bond with his two new 'sons.'

Early in the fall, Ron started saying that he'd love for us to take a vacation train trip across Canada. I thought it'd be a great surprise to give the trip to him for our anniversary the following September, but now it's too late, and it'll never happen.

We put our names on the waiting list of an adult retirement community. We had visited a previous pastor and his wife, who lived there, and were so impressed with the place. We were looking forward to someday getting the unit we wanted. It would have been big enough for everyone to stay with us for Christmas and other special occasions. Four months after Ron died, I got a call from the administrator saying they had a unit available for us. It wasn't the unit we had wanted, but it showed that we were at the top of the list, and our dream of moving there would become a reality in the near future. Now it's just my name on the waiting list, and I'm waiting for the call to go… but it'll only be me moving there… alone. I regret that we never got to move there together because we were so looking forward to living there.

Every morning, we had a routine. Ron was an early riser and during the off-season, when he wasn't working at the golf course, he still got up early. He used that time to read and pray. I'd walk out an hour or two later, we'd say our good mornings, and I'd go to the kitchen to make coffee. I always peeked into the living room and asked if he'd like coffee this morning. His response was usually, "Yes, thank you." I would bring it out to him when it was ready, and we would have it together. Five months after he passed away, I'd still look into the living room, see an empty chair and ask the silence if he wanted coffee this morning, and then I'd burst into tears as I received no response. Then, one morning the unthinkable happened! I walked out to the kitchen and made my coffee. All of a sudden it hit me! Oh my gosh! I walked out to the kitchen without looking at his empty chair, without saying good morning and asking if he'd like coffee. I can't begin to tell you the overwhelming guilt I felt that I'd forgotten our routine and was now just thinking of myself. I cried all day because I felt like I had betrayed him. It was devastating.

But by far, my greatest regret is that I didn't text Ron the night before his surgery to pray with him and tell him once more that I loved him. I could've told him that I followed him down to Southlake when they transported him there, but I never got to see him. I recall the trip to Southlake, and I have the parking stub to prove I was there. I remember waiting for the elevator and coming to the waiting room, but I never got to see him. Why did I not text him? Did he think I didn't come when I said I would? Did he think I didn't care?

Looking back on this, I now recognize that I was inflicting a sense of false guilt upon myself. It's very easy for false guilt to eat away at us. It becomes easy to fixate on what we didn't do and what we should've done. I'm learning that grievers can beat themselves up unmercifully with regrets and guilt. Because of the deep pain we're already experiencing, our minds and emotions can run wild, making a mountain out of a molehill. We place unrealistic expectations upon ourselves. But God isn't imposing guilt upon us, so why do we do it to ourselves? We evaluate everything we say and do. We evaluate everything we didn't say or do. *Why didn't I...? If only I had... We never got to... I meant to tell you... How could I forget to...? Why didn't I follow through on...? I should've... I could've... Why did I say that...? How did I miss...? I wish I had... I took that for granted... I didn't know what I had... It's all my fault.* The list goes on.

As Leanne Friesen writes, *"It may seem strange to need room to grieve things that technically don't exist, but this, too, is part of the grief process. We grieve the loss of dreams. We grieve the loss of things we had hoped for. We grieve anniversary parties that never happened, trips not taken, things not said... With loss comes regret. It is inevitable."*[17]

As grievers, we need to remind ourselves that we're not perfect and neither was the one we lost. We're human, and we've all come short on things we should've said or done. Sometimes the hardest

---
17. Leanne Friesen, *Grieving Room*: Minneapolis, MN, Broadleaf Books, 2024, 108.

thing for us to do is to forgive ourselves. We need to realize that this, too, is part of the grieving process. We need to recognize that God is the One who is ultimately in control. Our loved one's death didn't take Him by surprise. He's fully aware and fully present in our circumstances and wants to extend forgiveness and grace to us.

And that's the other side of the coin—forgiveness and grace.

What *is* forgiveness? It's releasing a debt—an offence—that the other person cannot pay. It's choosing to no longer feel anger or resentment toward someone or passing judgment on them because they hurt us or failed to live up to our expectations. It's an act of pardoning.

Shortly after Ron and I were married, one of the pastors at our church asked if he could borrow our car. His car was having work done on it at the garage, and he got an emergency call to go to the hospital to see someone. Ron loaned him our car. It was wintertime, and unfortunately, the pastor hit black ice. Thankfully, the pastor was okay, but our car ended up being totalled. My sister and brother-in-law loaned us money for a down payment on a new car. Each month, I'd give them a little at a time to help pay it off. Months later, I recall getting a 'receipt' of sorts from my sister, showing how much the debt was, how much we had paid down, and how much was still outstanding. At the bottom of the receipt were the words, *"Forgiven. Paid in full."* The debt of the outstanding balance was pardoned, and we were released from having to pay the rest. It was considered paid off and the debt was forgiven.

The griever often has the most difficulty forgiving themselves. Forgiveness is a choice we make. When we choose to forgive ourselves, we'll experience peace and no longer feel enslaved to the guilt we've imposed on ourselves. We need to understand that not everything we've said or done is something God is displeased with. Often, we take on His role as judge, pronouncing a guilty verdict on ourselves. If our regret is about something hurtful we said or did to someone, we can receive His forgiveness. Whether it's you or someone else you need to forgive for whatever reason, recognize that God has already paid your debt through Christ's death on the cross. Your sin was placed on Him, and He has paid the price for our sins—past, present, and future (Romans 6:10). We can walk in the freedom of His forgiveness. The proof of that is the grace we extend to ourselves and others.

Hanging on to guilt and regrets can be dangerous in the long run. If we allow it to fester in our hearts and minds, it can lead to isolation and depression. We need to recognize that God doesn't want us to live this way. He wants us to have an abundant life. He wants us to be at peace within ourselves, and He alone can give us that peace. Jesus promises to give us His peace. *"Peace I leave with you; My peace I give to you; not as the world gives, do I give to you. Let not your heart be troubled, nor let it be fearful."*[18] How is His peace different? He gives us peace through the presence of the Holy Spirit when we invite Him to take up residence in our lives. His peace is eternal, and it reassures us that

---

18. John 14:27 NASB.

He's in control. The world's peace is based on the circumstances surrounding us—on feelings tied to what's happening in our lives and around us. The world's peace is temporary and can shift in an instant. God's peace, however, is not based on the circumstances that surround us. It's based on His truth and His character. It's everlasting.

I was thinking about what must have been going through Ron's mind as he faced his surgery the night before and the morning of. Was he nervous? Apprehensive? Afraid? Who wouldn't feel that way? You're entrusting your life to the hands of a surgeon and medical team you don't know. Open heart surgery is not a trivial thing. But then I remembered what he texted his sister Glenda the night before. It was how he signed off on the text that caught my attention. Often, he would sign off with the words, "In His grip." He knew he was safe in his Father's hands. If I know him as well as I do, I believe he committed his life one more time into the grip of his Father as he was going into surgery. He would entrust his life to his Father's keeping, no matter what the outcome would be. If he survived the surgery, it would be a win, but if he didn't, it would still be a win because his faith would finally become sight. He knew being in the centre of God's will was the safest place to be. He would have no regrets with either outcome.

Those of us who grieve the loss of our loved ones, will experience regrets. Regrets and guilt are part of the grieving process, but we don't have to be bound to them for the rest of our lives. There is forgiveness, and because we've been forgiven, we can forgive others and ourselves. You're going through the worst experience of your life, so cut yourself some slack. Your loved one wouldn't want you to beat yourself up. Imperfect people do imperfect things. No one is exempt except for Jesus. Give yourself grace.

He already has.

The Gift of Grief

Chapter Eight

Irreplaceable Memories

Memories are treasured heirlooms forever cherished in our hearts.

I was about to get into my car one Sunday morning after church, when a woman I had known years ago from a previous church called out my name. I didn't know she was attending the same church as me. She asked how I was doing, and I asked her if she knew Ron had passed away. She said yes and that she prayed for me. Then, she told me there were two things she loved about Ron—his heart for others and his curly hair. We laughed.

Ron had gorgeous curly hair that the vast majority of men would've killed for. It was actually the first thing that attracted me to him. I'd sit in the choir beside my friend Anne, and before the service started, she'd lean over and whisper that he was sitting in the back row near the entrance. My eyes would immediately look for those golden brown curls, and when I found them, my heart would beat a little faster.

After we got married, I learned that Ron had a habit of wetting his hair with water every morning. He'd rub those curls, leaving water splashes all over the mirror. It drove me crazy that he didn't dry off the mirror, but instead, there'd be all these dried water marks for me to clean off. It was such a trivial thing, but it irked me. I even complained to the Lord about it, suggesting He tell Ron to wipe off the mirror! Did the Lord tell him to do that for me? No. Instead, He impressed upon me to be thankful that he was here to leave those splashes on the mirror for me to wipe off. And the interesting thing is—it never bothered me again.

At Ron's memorial, his sister Carol shared a story about how, in his younger days, Ron went to a Doobie Brothers concert at Massey Hall. He didn't feel that the crowd was giving them the kind of response they deserved. So he stood up on the second balcony and shouted, *"What the heck is wrong with you, Toronto?"* Thunderous applause apparently followed.

Part of my grief journey entails looking back over the years we had together and being grateful for all those things that serve as precious memories of who Ron was and what he did for us—for me. Ron had the gift of helps. That's why he was so good at his job at Bayview Glen for 34 years. He was responsible for a 66,000-square-foot building and its grounds. It was a huge responsibility to oversee the upkeep and ongoing maintenance of such a facility. He did set-ups and teardowns for in-house ministries, as well as for outside organizations that rented the church for their events. He had a vital role on the property committee, as everyone looked to him for his input and advice. He prepared the operational budget for the building maintenance, and met with suppliers, cleaners, and contractors. He was also responsible for all the operational building logistics for conferences, weddings, and funerals. He looked after the ongoing needs of the full-time daycare, which was part of Bayview Glen's ministry, and wrote up the monthly work schedules for those working with him. Nothing was ever beneath him.

Ron was the go-to person as our church grew in square footage, attenders, and ministry needs. Everyone agreed that he must've put in 10,000 steps a day—no wonder he was physically fit. He had two full-time assistants and at least eight to ten volunteers that he oversaw. Everyone said the same thing —he was always willing to help, and he did it with a smile on his face. He outlasted nearly all the staff that came and went during his employment. He was a good provider for our family.

Amid the demands of his job at Bayview Glen, Ron was a devoted family man. He was a hands-on dad—a 'park dad'. The girls loved going to the park with him when they were small. He played games with them and taught them how to ride their bikes. Every Canada Day, we'd spend the whole day celebrating together. He eventually 'buckled' under the tearful pressure from Brittany and me who both wanted a dog, and took us to see the cutest chocolate-brown dog—Buttons—who was advertised in the local pet store paper. Even at Brittany and Dave's wedding reception, he yelled out, *"Thanks for the dog, Brit,"* to which she responded, *"Thanks for walking him for me."* The place erupted into laughter.

He took the girls out driving when they were getting their driver's licenses. Holidays were special to him. He always took a picture of the dining room table after I decorated it for a special occasion. At Christmas, he'd make sure the 'fireplace' on TV was on while we opened stockings and gifts together. He even developed a liking for Shayla, our 50-pound dog, on Christmas Day. That was saying something, since most of the time he merely tolerated her. But she loved him. He was her faithful walker, and she loved her walks with him. The thrill of his life was walking our two daughters down the aisle. His girls were cared for, and he loved the two young men who stole their hearts. He had always wanted sons, and now he had two.

Ron grew up in Maple, Ontario, and it always held a very special place in his heart. He'd share all kinds of trivia about Maple with anyone who'd listen. Even at his memorial service, we learned that he shared his special memories of Maple with his work colleagues. In May 2023, there was a special Maple Reunion, and Ron was asked by the organizer to be the greeter as people arrived. He was thrilled to be asked.

Twice a year, Ron would organize a 'brothers breakfast,' and it quickly expanded to include the nephews and friends of his and his brothers. It eventually became a lunch get-together. Ron made all the arrangements—contacting everyone and keeping them posted on the final arrangements, booking the restaurant, and having the guys bring pictures that they reminisced about. The last one he organized took place exactly one week before he passed away.

On October 22, 2023, he took me to his workplace, Friday Harbour, to show me around the golf course. He was so proud of this place and the people he worked with. He got permission to have a golf cart to take me around the 18 holes. It was beautiful! He pointed out various things, like where he saw a deer one morning. He even had a picture of a coyote running across one of the greens. I'm so grateful for the memories we made on that afternoon together.

But, there's one memory that'll always stand out in my mind. Shauna was four years old at the time. Part of Ron's job was to open and close the church for the various occasions when it was used. Family Night was on Wednesdays. It was always a rushed evening for him to come home for dinner and then head back to open the church. This one particular night, when he was at the door ready to leave, Shauna burst into tears and said, *"Daddy. Don't go. Stay with me."* She'd never done this before, and she never did it again, but on this particular night, she needed her daddy, and he recognized that. He took off his coat and called one of the elders to ask if they could fill in for him because something had come up that required his attention. The elder said *"No problem."* In that moment, Ron saw the importance of meeting his little girl's need for him to be there for her and didn't hesitate to respond. They played together, and when it was bedtime, he tucked her in, read her a story, and prayed with her. I'm sure there will be a crown in Heaven for him because of that precious evening.

This chapter isn't merely one of reminiscing, but also one to show the importance of memories to those who grieve and how the church can help grievers remember and reminisce about their loved ones. Ask them about the dear one they've lost. Say their names. Let them tell you about them. This is so important to help them grieve and heal. We want and need to talk about our loved ones.

There are a number of ways we can commemorate our loved one's memory. One simple idea I heard is to create a memory jar by writing memories and character traits on pieces of paper and placing them in the jar. The idea is for you to read one of the pieces of paper each day so you can reflect and give thanks for a beloved quality or special memory—keeping them close to your heart.

For my family's second Christmas without Ron, I wrapped small boxes in Christmas paper. There was nothing in the boxes, but we each took one. Each box represented a particular memory or character trait about Ron that we cherished. We shared our special memories with one another and then put the boxes in

Ron's stocking so it wouldn't be empty. It had a profound impact on all of us, and everyone agreed that they wanted to make it an annual tradition.

There are a multitude of things that can be done to honour those special days on the calendar. It's so important to be sensitive on these occasions to those who grieve deeply. I began making it a practice to write down the date of those who've passed away on my calendar, so I could send a note or a text to their loved ones the following year to let them know I was praying for them. The anniversary of our loved one's death is often the hardest date of all. To know someone remembered that date speaks volumes to us and ministers deeply to our hearts. Make it a point to send them a note, a text or give them a call to let them know they haven't been forgotten and neither has their loved one.

We're forced to physically let go of our loved one and, for some of us, it feels like they were ripped away. For others, there may have been more time to prepare for their loved one's passing, but regardless, we all feel the weight of their sudden absence the moment they take their final breath. The real pain begins with the realization that our relationship with them is now gone. There's nothing we can do to bring them back or to 'buy more time'. Our love for them, however, never ends. Although the physical relationship is gone, the emotional relationship we shared is magnified. Grief enlarges our emotions, our love, our feelings, and our thoughts. Grief is the means of holding our loved ones close to our hearts.

Our memories memorialize those who've passed. Even family members that we never got to meet due to location or generational differences can hold a special place in our hearts. We can memorialize them. My sister and I have a great-grandmother whose name was Sophia Gilbert. She wrote poetry books that expressed her faith in God. My sister got to know her through her books and fell in love with her. She even has her picture displayed on a table in her living room. She has a special affinity for her and sees her as an inspiration and a mentor of sorts.

I'm so grateful that in the case of my parents and my husband, the last words we spoke to each other were, *"I love you."* I always think of this, especially on the dates of their passing. Ron and I cultivated this with our girls over the years. My daughters and I are very close and we connect nearly every day. Whether we're texting, on the phone, or on FaceTime, every conversation ends with us saying that we love each other. Even now, we're instilling that part of our legacy to my granddaughter, Haddie.

When I was reading Kenneth C. Haugk's book, *Journeying Through Grief Book 4, Rebuilding and Remembering*, he wrote, *"A woman who lost both of her parents in an automobile accident said, 'It may sound silly, but when I pray, I ask God to let my mom and dad know how much I still love them and miss them. It comforts me and helps me feel close to them.'"*[19]

I couldn't believe what I was reading because that's exactly

---

19. Kenneth Haugk, *Journey Through Grief: Rebuilding and Remembering Book 4*: St. Louis, MO, Stephen Ministries, 2004,2019, 22.

what I've been doing ever since my mom died in 2016, my dad in 2020, and now my husband. Every night, I ask Jesus to give them all a hug and a kiss from me and to tell them how much I love and miss them. I was so moved to think someone else does this, too. I talk to Ron's picture. I know he can't hear me, but it somehow helps me in my grief journey. Some have told me that when they visit their loved one's grave, they talk to them. We know they can't hear us, but it's a means of processing our grief. Our love for them doesn't die; it becomes stronger and more powerful than the death that took them away from us. It's a means of keeping their memory alive in our hearts.

Don't be afraid to ask a griever to tell you about their loved one. Ask how and where they met. Ask about their family. Ask what they did for a living. Ask if they have a favourite memory that stands out to them. Was there something they really loved to do or a place they loved visiting? If you knew their loved one, share a story or memory you have about them. A funny story is especially good because it's a well-known fact that laughter helps release endorphins. Endorphins are hormones that are released when we experience something pleasurable. They help to relieve stress and give a better sense of well-being, and can even reduce pain. Overall, they're mood-lifters. So, share those stories or sayings that you have of them. Grievers love to hear stories about their loved one that they may not have heard before. By doing this, you're helping us deal with our grief. If it brings tears to our eyes, please know that you didn't upset us. Remembering our loved one is helping us to grieve and to heal. They're worth remembering.

The Gift of Grief

Chapter Nine

The First Year - Dates in Memoriam

> *Maybe as time goes on, I will dread these special days less. Perhaps I can use them well and eventually they will bring joy instead of sadness. I choose to believe so.*[20]

The first year of bereavement is filled with hurdles that can't be dismissed or avoided: birthdays, anniversaries, Mother's Day, Father's Day, Christmas, New Year's, Easter, Thanksgiving, and other meaningful dates all mark special occasions and memories in our lives. The anniversary of our loved one's death and burial is the hardest of them all.

That first year is one of constant change for the person grieving. We've experienced an emotional kaleidoscope. One moment, we feel like we're okay, then seconds later, we're in a puddle of tears. We can't think straight, and decisions that we

---

20. Gary Roe, *Comfort for the Grieving Spouse's Heart*: Healing Resources Publishing, 2019, 159.

never gave a second thought become major hurdles for us. We then start to question if we're losing our minds.

I pride myself on being a detailed organizer, but when I lost my husband, I suddenly felt like I didn't know which end was up. My memory used to be sharp, but when Ron died, I felt like I couldn't remember anything. Dates for appointments, when bills needed to be paid, phone numbers, names of people I knew, and passwords were all impacted by the shock of my loss. Shock takes its toll for quite some time, creating brain fog for those grieving, which can last for a year, and in some cases, two years or longer. Our thought processes have been derailed by the intense grief that's overwhelmed us. We can't 'will' it back into working the way we need it to work. Unfortunately, there's no expiry date on grief, and each person's journey through this valley is unique to them, which includes the brain fog we experience. I can't begin to count the times I'd see or hear something and have a momentary flash, thinking, *I should tell Ron*, or *I should show this to Ron*. Approaching two years into my grief journey, I was still having those thoughts. This is perfectly normal.

The first Christmas without Ron was exactly one month after he passed away. It was like we were living in a shock bubble. I recall going into a store, and of course, they were playing Christmas music. All of a sudden, the song "I'll Be Home For Christmas" started to play, and I lost it. I tried to keep my head lowered so people wouldn't see the tears cascading from my eyes. When I went to the card section, the first card I saw said, *Merry Christmas to My Husband.* There I was again, rummaging through my purse, trying to find my Kleenex packet as the tears freely fell from my eyes. The same thing happened when my mom died. I was so embarrassed that the people around me saw me crying, so I left the store and went home.

Ron was your stereotypical husband who left his Christmas shopping until December. He always asked me to give him my list by the end of November. However, before he passed, he asked me at the beginning of November. I said I really didn't need anything, but I suggested something we could enjoy together while he was off for the winter. My biggest surprise was that he bought it in November. He also bought not one, but three Christmas cards for me, and inside one of them was the serviette from our wedding reception 41 years ago. I was reduced to tears. Even though he was gone, I still got one last Christmas present and cards from him. That meant the world to me.

Christmas has always been my favourite time of year. The tree goes up at the end of October, because I always felt we didn't get the full enjoyment of the season by putting the tree up mid-December. After Boxing Day, everything felt anticlimactic to me. Ron always helped me put the tree up, but then I'd decorate it with the girls. But that last year, he helped me decorate. It was as though he celebrated Christmas early with me.

Christmas was hard that first year. We were still in shock, so everything was low-key. Shauna, Brandon, and Haddie didn't come for Christmas as originally planned because they'd just made the trip three weeks earlier for the funeral. We didn't do stockings and gifts (although Brittany and Dave, Shauna and Brandon made me a stocking.) I just wrote cheques. We didn't do our family gift exchange when we were at Jeanne and Jim's for dinner. It just didn't feel right. I had mixed feelings about taking down the Christmas decorations. Normally, that wasn't an issue, but this would mark the last year Ron was there to enjoy them, knowing that he helped put them up. He loved turning off all the lights and just having the tree and Dickens Village lights on as he watched TV. Packing up the decorations and putting them away was like closing another chapter in my life. It hurt deeply. As for New Years—it was a wash. I had dinner with Jeanne and Jim, watched a movie, came home and went to bed early. I had nothing to celebrate.

Holidays and special occasions are so hard for the grieving because of the memories they evoke. Holidays are notably family times—getting together with those we haven't seen for a while and spending time with those we're close to. Death accentuates our loss all the more because that person is no longer there to celebrate with us, making their absence feel that much more intense.

Chronologically, the next hard date was Ron's birthday. He was born on January 31st, and Shauna wanted me to come and stay with her in Nova Scotia for his birthday. To honour the occasion, we went to a Swiss Chalet restaurant in Halifax because Ron loved Swiss Chalet. Brittany and Dave went to the Swiss Chalet in their neighbourhood at the same time and we texted back and forth. Though we couldn't be together physically, this was the next best thing. Everything was going well when all of a sudden, the happy birthday song erupted in another section of the restaurant. I lost it.

Valentine's Day was the next difficult date to navigate, as this was the day we got engaged. There are so many special memories associated with this day. It was a Sunday evening, and in those days, we still had an evening service at our church. My friend Myrna caught the sparkle on my finger prior to the service, and the next thing I knew, there was a huge crowd of people around me. Everyone was so excited that Ron and I were engaged. The pastor announced it in the service and everyone burst into applause and cheering.

Then there were birthdays—Shauna was in February, mine was in in April. Mother's Day came in May, and Father's Day followed in June. Each one of these occasions was difficult because we felt Ron's absence so deeply. Jeanne and Jim's 50th wedding anniversary was in the year following Ron's passing. They'd been planning a party for months, and Ron had been so looking forward to going. It was a time to celebrate, and yet, our family was grieving in the midst of it. I didn't want to take away from the joy of the occasion, but at the same time, I was grieving so deeply that Ron wasn't there with us. Friends of Jeanne and Jim put a digital photo presentation together. It never occurred to me that we'd be included. I was completely lost, staring at Ron in the pictures—I didn't see anyone else. Fighting back tears was a losing battle.

During dinner, the background music became a trigger for me. It was the same music Ron and I listened to while dating. Ron was a huge Gordon Lightfoot fan, so when I heard his songs playing, I told Brittany I had to leave the table. We stood outside the party room trying to pull ourselves together before rejoining the group. At the end of the evening, Dave and Jim were taking down the tables, and I heard Jim say that they weren't so easy to take down, which was another trigger for me. That was something Ron would've immediately known how to do, as he did it for 34 years at Bayview Glen. He was so missed!

When the girls were growing up, we celebrated Canada Day by playing mini golf, followed by ice cream. In the evening, we'd watch the fireworks. Brittany's birthday was in August—usually on or around the Civic Holiday. September is especially hard, as that's when we got married. There are so many wonderful memories from that day. We flew to Palm Desert, California, for our two-week honeymoon. October marked Thanksgiving, and the end of October was when I began preparing our home for the Christmas season.

The most difficult weeks of the year are November 20th to December 2nd. November 20th to 25th marked the beginning of Ron's heart issues in the hospital, leading up to his death on the 25th. December 2nd was Ron's burial and memorial service. Each month, those dates hit hard as painful reminders that he's no longer with us. But I found it wasn't just those dates that intensified my grief—it was also the days leading up to them that filled my heart with overwhelming dread and sadness.

There's an inexplicable sense of loss that begins to build as these special dates approach. The days and weeks leading up to them can create pain and discomfort. Grievers begin to dread their approach, feeling each wave and trigger that comes with the territory. Unfortunately, there's no predicting when the waves will hit us or what triggers will arise.

I mention all these dates to show just how many dates can be especially difficult for those who are grieving. There will be additional dates that hold significance for each person. It's important for those who haven't experienced this kind of loss to understand the ongoing nature of grief and how it continues to affect those of us who have lost a loved one. Every month carries its own significance, marked by pain that feels overwhelmingly emotional. This doesn't even take into account the everyday struggles of grief that bombard our thoughts and drain our energy. We're impacted from every angle by loneliness and sadness because we miss them so deeply.

When possible, it's good to have supportive people around us on those special days. It has been proven that planning something significant to mark the memory of our loved one on those dates can help bring healing to our hearts. There are so many things you can do to commemorate your loved one. It's totally up to the bereaved to decide what they'd like to do. Some may light a candle, while some may write a letter and read it on that special occasion. Others might plant a tree in their yard to honour their memory. If their loved one died of cancer, they might choose to run in a marathon. The Canadian Cancer Society organizes a number of different walks and marathons throughout the year in memory of those who've died from this dreadful disease. Others may decide to fund a scholarship in their loved one's name, and some may donate to a specific cause in their name or get a memorial tattoo. Some may even decide to take a mini vacation or visit their loved one's favourite spot. I know a gentleman who took eight of his wife's colleagues out for dinner in honour of her birthday. To mark the first year of my wedding anniversary without Ron, Brittany and I went to Friday Harbour, where Ron worked. He loved that place and the guys he worked with. We had lunch in the Club House and then visited with his boss and some of the guys Ron worked with. It was such a meaningful way to pay tribute to his memory.

One Sunday, as the ten-month anniversary of Ron's passing approached, I was deeply moved that the elder who prayed during the church service remembered several of us by name. It touched my heart as I was still new to the church. How we choose to mark these special dates is up to each individual. The important thing is that we remember them. Amid the tears, it brings comfort and healing to our hearts.

The Gift of Grief

Chapter Ten

When You Lose a Child

... weep with those who weep.[21]

I want to preface this chapter by acknowledging that I've never experienced the loss of a child, and therefore, I don't claim to be qualified to address this kind of grief. However, I have a number of friends who've experienced the death of a child, and I've been encouraged by them to include this as a chapter in this book. To all the parents reading this book who have lost a child, my heart goes out to you. There are simply no words to adequately speak of the excruciating pain and suffering you have endured and continue to experience.

The natural progression of life teaches us to believe that children will outlive their parents, so when a child dies, it's extremely hard to reconcile. Scripture tells us that children are a gift to us from God (Psalm 127:3). So why was this gift taken

---

21. Romans 12:15   NASB.

away? This was a child who was wanted, planned for, and loved before they were born. For you, as a mother-to-be, you felt their first kick. You marvelled at the ultrasound that showed you were carrying this new little one inside you. You wondered who they were and who they'd become. You questioned in your heart if you'd be a good enough mom to them.

As a husband, you shared in the joy of your child's development and their arrival with your wife. You had your own questions and feelings of inadequacy. Would you be a good father? Would you be a good example of how to live? Would you leave a lasting legacy that your children would want to follow? Would you be a good provider?

Both of you were excited about your child's arrival. You prepared the nursery and couldn't wait to bring your little one home with you. You bought baby clothes, baby furniture, baby toys, and your family and friends shared in the anticipation of the birth and safe arrival of your little one.

Years ago, two couples that Ron and I were friends with from our church were expecting their second child at the same time. Both of them tragically lost their babies. Linda and Andy's baby was a little girl, Emily, who died during the delivery because the cord was around her neck. Their loss was totally unexpected. Karen and Charles' baby, Bart, died minutes after he was born due to a serious abnormality. They'd been told a month before their baby's arrival that he wouldn't survive, as he wasn't growing.

During Karen's last month of pregnancy, people asked how she was feeling because it wouldn't be long before her baby was due. How do you respond? You know your baby isn't going to live, but nobody else knows. Bart lived for a few precious minutes following his birth. Charles and Karen's grief didn't begin in the delivery room, it began when they were told he wouldn't survive. What do you say? *This is not how it's supposed to be!*

My friend Pauline had a beautiful daughter named Paulanne, who was friends with Shauna and Brittany at school. Paulanne was a sweetheart in every way; she was even born on Valentine's Day. She loved music and loved to sing. She participated in the Bach Children's Chorus and the Bach Chamber Youth Choir. Paulanne died of cancer at the age of 22. Her mother told me that in her last moments, Paulanne asked her family if they could hear the singing she could hear. She said it was the most beautiful music she'd ever heard. She peacefully took her last breath and was ushered into the presence of God with angelic singing. I was asked to MC her funeral service, and Paulanne's high school and university friends participated as well. It was such a tribute to her life and her faith in Christ, but she left a huge hole in her family's heart. How does one survive and navigate through such pain and loss in the years following?

There are a million questions we can ask about losing children. There are simply no words that adequately describe the suffering of losing a child. They were part of you and you were part of them, and it leaves us asking, *"Why?"*

Why did God allow this to happen?

Why would God do this to me—to our family?

I asked God to heal my child, but He didn't. Why?

My daughter/son was a good person. Why did this happen?

When I cry out to God, I feel like He isn't there. Why does He feel a million miles away?

Why doesn't He care?

Why won't He take away my pain and suffering?

Why? Why? **Why?**

What is God's response to our questions of why? His answer is found in Isaiah 55:8-9 (NASB).

"For My thoughts are not your thoughts, neither are your ways My ways," declares the Lord. For as the heavens are higher than the earth, So are My ways higher than your ways, And My thoughts than your thoughts."

If we understood everything about God, we'd have no need for Him in our lives. But we don't understand everything about Him. We live in a broken world with broken people. Broken people with broken dreams of what could've been... but will never be now. Broken hearts that feel crushed under the weight of the pain and suffering they're forced to carry, and it's our brokenness that causes us to cry out to Him in desperation, *"Why?"*

When I asked my friends what the hardest part was about losing their child, their answers were strikingly similar: the absence of their presence, the sound of their voice and laugh, the cute idiosyncrasies of their personalities, their mannerisms and funny phrases, and the heartbreaking reality of not getting to watch them grow up. As one friend put it, *"Just knowing they were here with us was enough."*

One of the most difficult aspects of losing a child is the unfulfilled dreams parents have for their children. We all have great expectations for our children. We want them to be happy. We want them to be successful. We want them to be financially secure. We want them to have people in their lives to encourage them and challenge them to be all they can be. We want them to walk closely with God. We don't want them to experience hardship and loss. We certainly don't want them to suffer in any way—physically, mentally, emotionally, or relationally. We want the absolute best for them.

My dear friend Carol, a colleague at the school where I worked, lost her daughter Elizabeth to cancer in 2023, at the age of 34. Elizabeth was a vibrant and outgoing young lady who was so full of life. She had a long battle with brain cancer. Even though her family walked this road with her for a number of years, the reality of her death was no less painful than if she had died unexpectedly. She left behind two adorable little boys. Here's how Carol expressed her grief: *"There is a bond with your child that you don't have with your husband. You were joined together with your child by an umbilical cord. Elizabeth is a part of me, and I of her. There is a generational imprint, so to speak. That will never change. I mourn how I will never experience that growth in her that is also a part of me. The pain of her absence will be with me for the rest of my life."* The umbilical cord isn't just a physiological attachment between a baby and their mother for food and nutrients. There is also an emotional, spiritual, and genetic connection that contributes to who this little one will become.

So many children have been lost to death through disease, famine, drug overdose, suicide, and drunk driving. Far too often, we hear news stories about children who've drowned, who have been victims of human trafficking, or who have been abused and murdered. Many of us know people who've lost a child through miscarriage or during childbirth. Whether it's the loss of a young child, a teenager, or an adult child, the pain is still just as raw. The intensity of a parent's grief isn't determined by the age of their child. The pain of grief, suffering, and loss is heartbreaking. It defies description. A part of you has died with them because they've been and always will be a part of you. Unfortunately, life isn't fair and often leaves us with unanswered questions. Simply put, the death of a child doesn't make any sense.

This gives me food for thought—how many times have I asked God for a miracle that only He could do, but in the next breath, I'm setting the parameters of how I want and expect Him to answer? Then, when He doesn't answer the way I think He should, I try to make excuses for Him. If I'm really honest with myself, would I be satisfied if all my questions were answered? No, because they wouldn't change the circumstances or the grief of losing my loved one.

And yet, the Bible records story after story where God's glory shines the brightest during life's darkest moments. These stories highlight how God's purposes are so much greater than we can comprehend. One such story in John 11, tells about Lazarus. His sisters, Mary and Martha, sent word to Jesus, who was in another town, to come quickly because their brother was very sick. The Biblical account tells us that Jesus intentionally arrived four days after Lazarus had died and was buried. The sisters were distraught. Martha was angry and challenged Jesus, saying *"... if You had been here, my brother would not have died."*[22] Martha wanted to know why it took Jesus that long to come. It made no sense to her. Jesus actually told her that He was going to raise Lazarus from the dead, but she didn't understand that He was going to perform the miracle right before their eyes. She believed the resurrection of those who put their faith and trust in Him was to come in the future, not now.

When Mary met Jesus, she fell at His feet. She said the same thing as Martha, but her grief wasn't tinged with anger, as it came from a broken heart overwhelmed by sorrow and loss. Jesus was

---

22. John 11:21 NASB.

so moved and troubled by her deep grief and suffering that He responded to her sorrow with weeping (John 11:33-35). Many believe that Jesus cried because He loved Lazarus and was sad that His friend had died. Yes, He did love Lazarus, but I don't believe He cried because Lazarus had died. Jesus knew He was going to raise Lazarus from the dead. There was no reason for Him to cry. I believe Jesus cried in that moment because He saw the impact of death on mankind—one of hopelessness, and it grieved Him to tears. They couldn't see what He saw from eternity's perspective. He saw how people's lives had been shattered because of sin. He knew that the penalty for sin is death. He saw the hopelessness and grief that death caused. As my pastor put it, *"Jesus wept over death because He saw the effect it had on us. Death is a spiritual matter that has a physical effect."* We, too, feel the pain of suffering and loss that death has brought. We, too, like Mary and Martha, can't understand God's ways because they're so much greater than we can comprehend. We, too, can't see from eternity's perspective. Like Mary and Martha, we too want answers to our questions.

We may question why God has ordained for some to live longer than others and why some suffer greatly due to disease, but we may never know the answer to those questions. Deuteronomy 29:29 tells us, *"The secret things belong to the Lord our God, but those things which are revealed belong to us and to our children forever…"* If He's the all-powerful, omniscient and omnipresent God that we say we believe He is, can we not trust

Him with the unknown and unanswered issues that touch our lives? We trust Him with the good things. Can we trust Him with the bad, the painful, the unanswered, the unknown? We pray for God to remove suffering from our lives, but what if He wants to teach us valuable lessons that can only be learned in the crucible of our pain and suffering? His purposes are always good. Do we believe that? In faith, can we trust Him with our pain, our loss, our suffering, our broken hearts, when nothing makes sense to us? Are we willing to trust that He never wastes any of our experiences?

We always see things more clearly looking back in hindsight, don't we? Yet God wants us to look forward, putting our complete faith and trust in Him. The truth is, He doesn't always answer the way we want or hope. We aren't exempt from the pain and suffering of this imperfect world, but neither was His Son. Jesus wasn't exempt from the pain and suffering He endured on the cross, even though He pleaded for that cup to be removed from Him. The big difference is that Jesus said, *"Father, if it is Your will, take this cup away from Me; nevertheless not My will, but Yours, be done."*[23] He didn't propose a Plan B, but instead submitted Himself to the outcome of His Father's will. Again, I'm challenged and humbled by the reality of what total surrender and trust look like.

The people whose stories I've shared with you are ordinary people like you and me; however, to me, they're giants of the faith. Though they don't have all the answers to their questions, they

---

23. Luke 22:42 NKJV.

still place their full confidence and trust in the One whose purpose is for them to become a reflection of His Son in the midst of their pain. That ultimately brings glory to God, and through their tears of heartache and grief, they whisper, "...*Nevertheless, not my will, but Yours, be done.*"[24]

---

24. Ibid. NKJV.

Part Three

GRIEF

The Teacher

The Gift of Grief

Chapter Eleven

Change is Inevitable

Jesus Christ is the same yesterday, today, and forever.[25]

Change. Change is a fact of life. Nothing stays the same. We don't always like change, especially as we get older. You've probably heard the old phrase, *"But we've always done it this way."* There's comfort in routine and when something unexpectedly throws a wrench into that, it can feel very disruptive and invoke feelings of dis-ease.

That's what grief does. It throws a wrench into our lives. It changes our direction. It's like driving in the dark of night, and all of a sudden, there's a detour sign. We have no choice. Although we weren't anticipating this, we must readjust to our new surroundings, which is always harder in the dark. All of a sudden, whether we like it or not, we're forced to go in a new direction—it's not an option.

---

25. Hebrews 13:8 NKJV.

Grief is like a detour sign. It changes our circumstances, our responsibilities, our relationships, our routines, and our life goals. It changes **us**! We've been thrown into an unimaginable situation, and we're forced to take a new perspective. We're obligated to make the necessary adjustments whether we want to or not. It isn't just the loss of our loved one that we grieve. That alone is more than we can bear. No, it's the additional losses that are associated with our loved one that add to the pain of their absence. Now we have to begin to see our life through a different lens, which can be scary and uncomfortable.

One of the changes I struggled with was no longer being part of a couple and realizing that it's now just *me*. You don't realize when you're married how intertwined your identity is with your spouse. It's part of becoming one with them. Yes, we were individuals, but we were united together as one, and that union has now been severed.

One aspect of no longer being a couple that I found difficult concerned my wedding rings. I noticed a friend had taken her wedding rings off, but I don't want to take mine off. Our wedding rings were our wedding gifts to each other. They represent the love we have for each other. I even tried putting Ron's ring on with my rings, but his is too big and I'm not ready to resize it. A friend knew I was struggling with this, so she assured me that there's no reason to feel I had to take them off. It's my choice, and her reassurance gave me a sense of relief.

During our 41-year marriage, Ron and I had specific responsibilities. We never sat down and said, *"Okay, you look after this and I'll take care of that."* We just grew into them. In addition to working full time, he looked after everything pertaining to the car—from tire changes, maintenance, and repair appointments, to washing it. The garage was automatically his domain. He cut the grass, looked after all the gardening, and cleared the driveway in the winter. He oversaw all the upkeep and maintenance of the garden tools and snowblower. He kept his tools in an organized fashion so he knew where they were when he needed them. He organized the storage of anything else that needed to be looked after seasonally. Inside the house, he took responsibility for the furnace, air conditioning, buying salt for the water softener, and booking maintenance calls. He also walked the dogs.

I looked after more of the domestic responsibilities in addition to working—meals, grocery shopping, cleaning, looking after the family budget, overseeing the house renos we had done, buying plants and shrubs for the property, hospitality and entertainment, and taking the dogs to their veterinary appointments. My outside commitments involved having a music ministry in churches. I also led Women's Ministries in the church for over 35 years, which required overseeing a team as well as organizing meetings and outreach events. If I were pressed for time, Ron would take on some of my household responsibilities. We both shared in the parenting of our girls. When I look back now, I see what a huge adjustment his absence has brought into my life.

One thing I wasn't prepared for was how losing a spouse would change some of the relationships we had shared with others. Some who we had considered friends, all of a sudden disappeared into the background. They didn't know how to relate to me as a single person. With a few, it happened right after the funeral; with others, it was a gradual loss of contact.

Grief is uncomfortable for those who've never experienced it on a deep level. They're often at a loss for words and don't know how to respond to us. They see us as the ones who've changed, and yes, that's true, but what they fail to recognize is that their approach to relating to us has also changed. All of a sudden, they feel nervous or uncomfortable around us and are afraid they might upset us. We did things together as couples, but things have changed, and I'm no longer 'a couple.' What should they do about that? They don't understand that withdrawing only creates more pain and increases my loneliness. That's why it's crucial for the church to understand the importance of coming alongside those in the midst of grief. The GriefShare group has become a precious group for me to connect with. They understand the pain of loss and are there for each other. They've become a new group of friends.

Everyday routines Ron and I shared are now gone. Going for coffee, having conversations about something we read or heard in the news, tackling a project together, taking a drive to see the Christmas lights or fall leaves, going for a walk along the

Boardwalk—they're now all distant memories. For some, it might be going to the gym together, going out for dinner every week, or golfing. The loss of all these times together creates an emotional upheaval in our lives.

Life goals are also impacted. As a couple, we had our way of doing things and an idea of what we planned or wanted to do further down the road. Goals we had together have now changed. Some goals I may be able to pursue on my own, but some I've had to abandon altogether. The good news is I can set new goals for my life because it's part of moving forward.

The year 2020 marked the beginning of an unexpected global season of grief. COVID took over the world. With the exception of a few islands in the Pacific and Atlantic Oceans, there wasn't one person on the face of the earth who wasn't impacted by the pandemic in some way. There hadn't been anything like it in 100 years, and it threw the world into a tailspin. Leaders frantically tried to figure out what started it, how it became so widespread, and how they'd attempt to combat it. Loved ones were isolated from those who were suffering from the disease. Thousands died alone without the love and support of their families because they weren't allowed to be with them in their last days. It had an impact on everything that touched our lives—the economy, investments, food chain supplies, the stock market, the real estate market, and gas prices. Surgeries were cancelled, and it was difficult to obtain medical help. We all watched businesses in our towns and cities struggle to stay afloat, but many succumbed to closure because they couldn't survive. It was an unprecedented time of pain, suffering, and loss.

Grief makes us question, *How will I survive my loss? How will I survive my future?* My life changed the moment I was told Ron was gone. Our hopes and dreams dissolved into thin air. The biggest detour of my life confronted me, and I had no clue which way I was supposed to turn. I felt like the darkness of my loss was choking me. Overwhelming feelings of, *'I can't handle this! I don't know what to do now!'* flooded my mind. I felt like I'd been thrown overboard into an ocean of grief, tossed around by massive waves that threatened to swallow me. How does *anyone* survive this?

Grief doesn't just overwhelm us emotionally. We experience major changes physically as well. It engulfs our entire being. Psychotherapist, Megan Devine points out, *"Studies in neurobiology show that losing someone close to us changes our biochemistry: there are actual physical reasons for your insomnia, your exhaustion, and your racing heart. Respiration, heart rate, and nervous system responses are all partially regulated by close contact with familiar people and animals; these brain functions are all deeply affected when you've lost someone close. Grief affects appetite, digestion, blood pressure, heart rate, respiration, muscle fatigue, and sleep… If it's in the body, grief affects it… cognitive changes, memory loss, confusion, and shortened attention spans are all common in early grief. Some effects even last years—and that's perfectly normal."*[26]Our bodies are truly miraculous. To try and understand how all the parts of our body work in conjunction with one another is beyond comprehension. When one part is impacted in a negative way, the body gets to work trying to compensate for it.

There's no training manual to teach us ahead of time how grief will throw our lives out of balance. There's no course that can teach us how to grieve before we're unexpectedly hurled into it. We basically get thrown into the deep end of the pool, totally overwhelmed by our new surroundings, wondering how we can break through the surface to breathe. Unfortunately, even if we think we can prepare ourselves for that fateful day, the truth is, we can't. No one can anticipate how they'll respond when confronted with death. No one can project the circumstances that'll fling us headlong into pain and suffering that defy anything we've ever encountered. Yet, as we flail in the deep waters of grief that threaten to drown us, there's a lifeline. For me, it was the strength of my faith in Christ, as well as the prayers and support of family and friends, that carried me so I could finally make it to the surface and catch my breath.

---

26. Megan Devine, *It's OK That You're Not OK*: Boulder, CO, Sounds True, Inc., 2017, 117

… The Gift of Grief

Chapter Twelve

There's Nothing Normal About My 'New Normal'

I have today to live the best I can.

I'm an organizer. I'm a detail-oriented person. I like routine. I make appointments. I live by my calendar. I follow a plan when I'm going to do something. I'm a creature of habit. This is all normal and predictable for me. The word 'normal' conveys the idea that something is done as usual, as expected and is typical. That was pretty much me.

Then, everything changed. The predictable became unpredictable. My world turned upside down. I felt like I was drowning in quicksand, and no matter how hard I tried, I couldn't get out of it. I was aware of my brain trying, but unable to process the worst news of my life. Everything was so surreal. My emotions were all over the map. And if that wasn't bad enough, I felt bombarded by multiple emotions all at once—anguish, confusion, crying, and feeling totally overwhelmed. I questioned if I was losing my mind, and I felt actual pains in my chest from the deep loneliness I was experiencing. I was heartbroken, and I couldn't focus on anything but my loss. It was a depth of sorrow I've never experienced before and never want to experience again. I wondered what would happen next, and how I'd manage. My life was abruptly interrupted, and I couldn't figure out what to do. No matter how hard I tried, I couldn't recall events surrounding Ron's death. They were, and still are, veiled in my memory.

Then there's the brain fog. Wow! I'd heard of this before, but now I was living it. People would say something to me, and it went in one ear and straight out the other. I couldn't focus or concentrate if my life depended on it. My attention span was dramatically shortened. It affected my whole being—emotionally, physically, mentally, spiritually, and socially.

I liken brain fog to a plane flying through thick clouds. You can't see anything around you. You have to entrust your life to the pilot and all the flight controls he has in the cockpit to navigate the plane. It isn't until the clouds finally dissipate that you can move forward with a clearer vision of what lies ahead. I'd explain this to people and ask them to bear with me. I looked to each new day with the hope that the fog might've lifted, but it didn't. So I'd hope that maybe it would be lifted tomorrow instead. There have been a lot of anticipated 'tomorrows' regarding my brain fog. It was just one more thing that caused me to throw myself on the Pilot of my life to get me through the clouds of confusion. As I look back, I see small signs that those clouds are slowly dissipating and because of that, I take heart. I still have a ways to go. It's a very disarming experience, to say the least.

What we don't realize is how hard our brains work to handle all the trauma and sadness. I like how Megan Devine describes it. *"… our minds work by creating new relationships and recognizing patterns. New information comes in, and the brain connects it to what we already know. Normally this process is seamless… In grief, your brain has to codify and collate an impossible new reality into itself. The data presented doesn't make any logical sense. There has never been anything like this event, so there is no way to connect or relate it to anything else. It doesn't fit. The brain cannot make the new reality fit… Those blips and gaps in your memory and thought processes are the brain trying to make the data fit into a world that cannot absorb that data. Eventually, it will understand that this loss can't fit inside the structures that used to be. It will have to make new pathways, new mental relationships, wiring this loss into the person you are becoming every day. You aren't crazy. You aren't broken. Your brain is busy, and it will simply take a while to come back online… Your mind… will adapt. This loss will be absorbed and integrated."*[27]

---

27. Megan Devine, It's OK That You're Not OK: Boulder, CO, Sounds True, Inc., 2017, 129-130.

When I was growing up, our family moved a lot. In the early years, my dad was a builder. We always knew when we were going to move because he'd finish the basement. He was always monitoring the real estate market to see when it was the most advantageous time to put the house up for sale. As a result, I went to seven different elementary and secondary schools. I remember how I hated going to a new school and having to make friends all over again. Fortunately, it wasn't an issue for me since I'm an extrovert, but I hated the process of saying goodbye and starting all over again. Now I'm faced with leaving behind the 'normal' I've grown accustomed to. Now I'm faced with having to walk into an unknown future. Now I'm having to start over, walking alone. It was so much easier and comforting to walk with the one I loved, rather than by myself.

I've been cast into this valley of loss, and behind me is my *old normal*. On the other side of the valley that lays ahead of me is what's often referred to as my *new normal*. I didn't want to embark on this journey; I wanted to go back to my old life because it was comfortable and familiar. It was my happy place. My new normal feels like a foreign land. I don't like the landscape. It feels barren, like it lacks the life, colour, and vibrancy of my old normal. There's a heaviness in the air, and the people there look just like I feel—stuck in a new normal that they didn't choose. They too look and feel tired. They look like they haven't had a good night's sleep in months. I can relate. For over a year, I was awake at all hours of the night, replaying everything over and over in my mind. It was disruptive and exhausting. I started wondering if there was a deeper issue preventing me from sleeping. I was encouraged by Gary Roe in his book, *Grief Walk*. I learned, *"Many grieving hearts report that nighttime is difficult. We lay our heads on the pillow and our minds flow to where our hearts are—with our loved one. Our thoughts begin to race faster and faster. Waking up to an anxiety attack is not uncommon. Our minds and hearts are processing our pain and grief, even while we sleep."*[28] As I speak with some of my fellow grievers in my new normal, we share how the waves and triggers continue to rain down on us as we adjust to our new life. We also share that we talk to our loved ones' pictures. We talk to ourselves. We can't stand the silence, it's deafening. A number of us said we couldn't eat at our tables by ourselves for the first year. Some still can't after a number of years. Will this always be a part of our *new normal?*

There's a choice to make. We can stay in the valley of loss and grief or we can begin to climb up the hill to give our new normal a shot. Obviously, it isn't our first choice; however, it's the better choice out of the two options since we'll never be able to go back to the way things were.

My new normal means creating a new routine. It means I now make dinner for one, not two. I do laundry for one, not two. I go grocery shopping for one, not two. When I go somewhere in the

---

28. Gary Roe, *Grief Walk:* Healing Resources Publishing, 2020, 150.

car, I go by myself. When the car needs a gas fill-up or repairs, it's me who looks after it. I no longer buy gifts for the one who meant the world to me. When I watch something on TV, it's my choice, not his. I don't go to restaurants anymore unless I'm going with family or if a friend invites me. There's no more treating each other to a Tim Hortons coffee. I miss having those unscripted conversations with him throughout the day. There were times we could finish each other's sentences. The things I'd ask him to help me with, I now have to do by myself because no one's here to ask. Ron always came to my rescue when the lid on a new jar was too hard to open, if there was a screw in the wall that came loose, or if the smoke detector needed new batteries. But these are now my responsibilities. He never let me pull out the totes of Christmas decorations from the storage room, but that's my job now. I no longer get phone calls, emails, or text messages from him during the day. Ron used to empty the dishwasher and wind the grandfather clock. Now, it's me. For the first ten months after he passed, I slept across the bottom of our bed because I couldn't bear to see his side of the bed empty. I still pile all the pillows and shams on his side.

    I bought a large grocery cart because it's no longer the two of us sharing the load and carrying the bags together. I now open and close my car door by myself after I get in. I no longer get phone calls from anyone asking to speak with Ron. When I see a couple holding hands or kissing as they walk together, it crushes me. I miss him holding my hand. I miss that kiss that said he loved me. I'm trying to come to terms with speaking in the singular (me) as opposed to the plural (we). I have to walk in my new normal, and Ron isn't there walking with me. I now walk alone and it really hurts.

I never realized how alone one could feel in a crowd, but now I do. I never recognized the extent to which our lives were intertwined. Yes, we were one, but we were also individuals. I gave him the space to be with his guy friends, just as he did for me with my girlfriends.

I spoke with a woman whose husband died five years ago. She shared how even now, there are moments when she wishes she could die because she questions the value of her life now that her husband is gone. Yet, she bravely gets up every morning looking for ways to live her life with a sense of purpose.

Another woman I spoke with lost her husband to cancer five years ago, and the idea of getting married again is a total turn off. *"No one will ever replace him!"* she says. A pastor at my church lost his first wife a number of years ago. He ended up meeting and marrying a woman who lost her first husband years before. They've been married for 16 years as I write this, and they're so grateful that they found love again. I recall hearing that he spoke to a group and shared how they'd talked about whether they should get married, knowing that one of them would eventually have to walk through the valley of death and suffering again. Could they do that? Were they willing to do that? It's a 50/50 chance that they could be the one left standing alone again. While going through the grieving process, it's strongly advised not to pursue another relationship. For some, the possibility of remarriage isn't an option. For others, it may be. Neither choice is right or wrong because it's a deeply personal decision.

No one can predict how the future will unfold. When we try to plan for the future, we don't include plans for sickness or loss. We look through rose-coloured glasses. When we're young, we see the happily ever after that we want. However, we all know that isn't how life works. We live in a fallen world with unrealistic dreams and imperfect people. Things don't always turn out the way we hoped they would.

Who would ever ask for a life of pain and suffering, whether it's through sickness or loss? We can become overwhelmed with fear and question what tomorrow holds and how we'll manage it. Grief does the same to us. It leaves us floundering with unanswered questions, disappointments, and removes all sense of order. The difference is that grief consumes our attention and magnifies our new reality. With grief, we ask the same questions— only with a different, and dare I say, more focused perspective. Life becomes more real, more prioritized, …more sacred. We see how precious life really is and are now learning not to take it for granted the way we used to. Starting to live our new normal takes every bit of the courage and energy we have. Gary Roe describes it well. *"Grief is an earthquake in the heart. The aftershocks continue. You'll be experiencing them for a while. Life may feel shaky and uncertain. Now you're faced with not only huge loss, but massive rebuilding. That won't happen quickly. Don't get in a hurry. This isn't a sprint. As you focus on grieving well, you'll be able later to handle the challenges of remaking the future – one step at a time."*[29]

Although I don't walk in this life with Ron anymore, I don't walk alone. I carry his memory in my heart and always will. Although he's not with me physically, he'll never be forgotten. People who are further ahead of me in this journey—in their new normal—have told me the pain lessens gradually over time, but a sadness will still remain. I'm told that I'll find peace in the memories I carry. The special dates I hold in my heart will stay with me like precious heirlooms of days gone by. There will be smiles. There will be tears. There will be sighs. There will also be peace, hope and yes, even joy as I walk in this new land. So, I choose to let the One who holds my life in His hands lead me, walk with me, and teach me new lessons that I wouldn't have had the privilege of learning if not for this journey through grief.

---

29. Gary Roe, *Heartbroken:* Wellborn, TX, GR Healing Resources, 2015, 89.

The Gift of Grief

Chapter Thirteen

Help! What Do I Say?

A soothing tongue is a tree of life.[30]

Ron and I attended a life group at the church. Some of the group members lived in our condo building, so we knew them as neighbours. A few weeks after Ron passed away, I was parking my car and noticed that a couple from our life group was parking their car as well. We started walking toward each other and I could see the wheels turning in Jim's head. *"What do I say to her?"* As we got closer, he suddenly stopped, opened his arms, embraced me with a big bear hug and said, *"I don't know what to say."* I told him he didn't have to say anything. The hug was more than enough.

When we encounter someone who is experiencing a difficult situation in their life, we often feel we have to say something that'll somehow make things better. We want to have answers for them, but the truth is, we don't have answers because there aren't any.

---

30. Proverbs 15:4 NASB.

When we grieve the loss of someone dear to us, the depth of pain we feel is unlike anything we've experienced before. We know that no one can alleviate it for us. What we desire is love from people who will walk with us and not try to 'fix' us. Grief isn't something that can be fixed; it's not a problem to be solved. It's a journey that we must walk through. Your care and support are the greatest gifts you can give us.

My dear friend and mentor, Gerry, is now 94 years old. Back in 1984, her first husband, Jim, died of a heart attack on Father's Day. He was 62 and Gerry was 52. It was an unimaginable shock for Gerry and her three children. Gerry recalled how a dear lady came up to her at the funeral and said, *"At least you know where he is."* Five years later, tragedy struck again. It was Canada Day and Gerry's daughter, Wynelle, was coming off a midnight shift at the Foothills Hospital in Alberta. She fell asleep at the wheel of her car and was killed instantly in a tragic accident. Once again, a well-intentioned soul said to Gerry, *"At least you have two other children."*

Both of these people had good intentions and weren't saying these things to cause more pain for Gerry. The first one spiritualized her husband's death and the second one thought reminding her that she still had two other children would bring a sense of peace that she wasn't alone. However, nothing could've been further from the truth. Her response to the first woman was, *"Yes, I know where he is. But I also know where he isn't—he isn't with me."* When I asked Gerry how she answered the second woman's comment about having two other children, she said she walked away without speaking. I totally understand that.

We're not grieving that our loved one is out of pain or that he/she has gone to be with the Lord. We grieve the loss of that person's presence and love. Their absence creates such an emptiness and loneliness. The relationship we once enjoyed with them is gone, and that's what hurts so deeply. Our grief is born out of our love for them. Again, I'm reminded of the importance of putting ourselves in someone else's shoes to gain a better understanding of what they're experiencing.

For the most part, I believe that people want to support and comfort those who've lost a loved one, but for some reason, many end up acting like a deer in headlights, and their minds go blank. They don't know what to say, so they avoid us and don't say anything. They don't realize how isolating that is. Grievers are in such a vulnerable place and are desperate for connection. Please don't avoid us, talk to us!

Again, the purpose of this book is to assist the church by giving them tools so they can come alongside those who grieve during their time of distress and need. I've had people tell me that they don't know what to say or do to comfort someone grieving. They've asked me what kind of responses and actions I appreciated when I lost Ron. I found the following responses to be comforting:

"I'm so sorry."

"Can I give you a hug?"

"I'm praying for you."

"I can't begin to imagine the pain (shock) you're experiencing right now."

"I love you."

"I don't know what to say."

"My heart goes out to you right now with all you've gone through."

"My heart really hurts for you."

"I really miss Ron. I so appreciated _____ about him." (They'd comment on his heart to help others, or another action or character trait of his.)

"I'd like to help you in any way I can." (Suggest something you could do to help. Please follow through on this. We look forward to it and see it as a promise to help.)

The greatest gift someone can give is sometimes silence and a hug or a squeeze of the hand. Hugs can actually reduce anxiety, stress hormones, and give a sense of connection. Be mindful about whether the person likes to be hugged or not.

A Recap of Things to Remember About Grievers:

Until you've walked the painful journey of grief, suffering, and loss, you cannot fully understand or identify with the pain that the bereaved face. There are a number of things to remember about those who are mourning the loss of a loved one.

1. **No two people grieve the same.** Grief is unique to each person. Husbands, wives, men, women, and children all grieve differently from each other. Some may be more extroverted, sharing everything they're feeling, while others may be introverted and keep their emotions to themselves. Grievers need people around them who won't compare them to someone else's situation and how they handle grief.

2. **There's no set time frame for grieving.** Each person grieves in their own time and their own way. Grief cannot be rushed. I remember finding a robin's nest in one of our shrubs as a child. There were two eggs left in the nest. One looked like it was starting to crack, and I recall my mother telling me NOT to break the shell so the baby bird could come out. That sounded cruel to me! Why wouldn't I help a weak and struggling creature? I learned that the bird's struggle to break out of the egg on its own was actually what helped to build its strength to eventually learn to fly. Similar to that bird fighting its way out of the shell, our struggle with suffering and death can actually help make us stronger to face the world.

3. **Grievers need and want to talk about their loved ones.** It's part of the healing process. It's crucial for us to talk about our loved ones and their deaths. Your gift of quietly listening and validating our feelings means the world to us because it shows that you aren't there to 'fix' us. There may be times we want to talk and other times we won't. Be sensitive to that. It's important to respect a griever's boundaries, as there may be things we're not ready to discuss.

4. **Grievers need your empathy.** A griever's life has been catapulted into a whole new world and direction. It's a journey full of changes, adjustments, questions, and the unknown. It affects everything we do. We never asked to walk this valley. It's hard and exhausting mentally, physically, emotionally, and spiritually.

5. **Grievers experience emotional waves and triggers.** These can overwhelm us at any time. It could be seeing a greeting card in a store, smelling a fragrance, or hearing a song on the radio. All of a sudden, the floodgates open, and there's no stopping the tears. There's no limit to what can trigger feelings of sadness in a brief moment. As hard as these are to endure, they're actually a necessary part of the grieving process. We desperately need people to understand the power those emotions exert over us. We need your support and encouragement when they overtake us.

6. **Grievers experience brain fog.** This can be one of the most unsettling parts of grief that can last for two years or longer. We can't remember things that were said to us—appointment dates, passwords, people's names, or directions. You name it, we'll forget it. It's extremely frustrating for us, so please give us grace during this time.

7. **Grievers can never go back to the way they were.** Due to the circumstances we've been thrown into, we've changed. We don't like it, but it's our new reality. Our loss has changed us and our lifestyles. We have to adjust to a 'new normal'. Having people who understand that our lives have dramatically changed, while still supporting us, is truly a gift.

8. **Grievers hate to cry in front of you.** The first thing many of us will do is apologize for our tears. We don't want to make others feel uncomfortable. It's important for us to cry without apologizing. Our tears are an expression of our love for the one we've lost. Please encourage us not to apologize when the tears start flowing.

9. **Grievers can't handle expectations placed on them.** We're so overwhelmed by our circumstances and emotions in the process of trying to deal with everything we're experiencing, that our bodies and brains have gone into overdrive. It's exhausting and upsetting. We truly appreciate not having expectations placed on us.

10. **Grievers need stability.** Everything in our lives has been touched by our loss. Our relationships with our loved ones were a source of stability, and many of us feel that that has been ripped away, making us feel like we've lost our footing. We're left trying to navigate through unknown territory, which can be very destabilizing and unnerving. So, having someone bring calm and stability into our lives by their very presence and support, is a priceless gift to us.

We know there's nothing that can be said to bring our dear ones back or to lessen the pain, but knowing people love us and are praying for us is comforting. What we miss most about our loved ones is their presence in our lives. The loneliness is more than we can bear at times. As grievers, to know people are willing to stand with us and be present in our lives is a huge blessing. To know they are willing to invest their time in our lives and journeys through grief is a major part of healing. It's truly a gift.

The Gift of Grief

Chapter Fourteen

Oops! I Shouldn't Have Said That!

Like apples of gold in settings of silver is a word spoken in right circumstances.[31]

Hoof-in-mouth disease. We've all experienced it at one time or another. We said something and as soon as it was out of our mouths, we felt the heat of embarrassment and regret colour our cheeks. We immediately chastise ourselves for saying (or doing) such a stupid thing. For the rest of the day, our minds replay what we said and we silently beat ourselves up for it. The unfortunate part comes when people say something and don't recognize that it was in poor taste or untimely. Unfortunately, there have been times when people's words have not been a comfort to me. Their words have lacked thought and sensitivity. Here are some examples of unfortunate things people have said to me and to other grievers I know.

---

31. Proverbs 25:11 NASB

1. **I know how you're feeling**. No one can say they know how another person feels. Grief is very personal and unique to each of us. You didn't have the same relationship I shared with that person. You can't possibly know the grief I'm experiencing. This also opens the potential for you to take over the conversation with your own story. Don't go there!

2. **Just let me know if you need anything or want to talk.** Someone wrote this in a condolence card to me. Being in shock and just trying to keep my head above water was so overwhelming. So, having to think of something for you to do, for me, felt like the tipping point. Take the initiative. Chances are, there are errands that need to be run. Certainly, preparing meals aren't top of mind for us.

   My son-in-law, Dave, came up on the day Ron died and sat with me on the sofa. We cried together and talked. Suddenly, he got up and went into the kitchen. I could hear him opening cupboards and the fridge, and it hit me, *"Oh my gosh! He's hungry. I should've made him lunch!"* He came out of the kitchen a few minutes later, carrying a plate with cheese, crackers, and fruit on it for *me*. He wasn't making it for *himself,* he was thinking of *me*. Another way you can help, especially if the bereaved live in a house, is to cut their lawn or do some gardening for them.

These aren't at the top of our priority list when we are overwhelmed with grief, but they're a huge help to us.

3. **How are you doing?** I have mixed emotions about this question. Personally, I see it as showing that someone cares about how I'm coping, but there are others who view this as insensitive. Some have told me that when they were asked this question, they wanted to respond with sarcasm and throw it back in their faces, asking, *"How do you think I'm doing?"* If in doubt, avoid asking this question! It's better to err on the side of caution.

4. **He or she had a long/full life.** The pain of grief is about separation from the one who died. Age isn't a factor in our grief. Our hearts hurt because we miss their presence in our lives. This statement has the potential of sending a subliminal message that our loved ones' lives were more than adequate and therefore we shouldn't need to grieve so deeply.

5. **At least they're not suffering anymore...** That's true, but we are suffering the loss of them. Of course, we're grateful and relieved that they're no longer in pain, but we're left trying to deal with the massive holes in our hearts that their absence has created.

6. **They're in a better place.** We know where they are. As my mentor shared with me, *"The issue isn't where he*

is, it's where he isn't. He isn't with me." Again, our grief is focused on the absence of people we love, being taken from us.

7. **You'll move on.** Move on from what? Move on from where? To 'move on' expresses the idea of leaving behind and abandoning someone or something. It's unfathomable for us to think we'd be capable of leaving our loved ones behind. Society is so uncomfortable with death and pain because they can't control it. They see the next best thing is trying to get away from it by moving on as soon as possible.

8. **You're young enough, you can get remarried.** We, as grievers, don't think about that, nor do we want to. Our immediate response is that no one will replace our loved ones. Suggesting that implies that our loved ones are to be forgotten and are replaceable. It makes us feel like our loved ones are no longer important because they're gone.

9. **Time heals all wounds.** First, we don't need clichés; and second, time doesn't heal all wounds. Over time, as we adapt, the pain may become less severe, but the wound is still there and always will be. God never intended for grief to be something we get over. It's a response of love for the one we lost. You can't squeeze that into a time frame because we'll carry them in our hearts forever. *"Grief comes in waves, not cycles or predictable patterns. And so time has little effect on the overall nature of our*

sorrow… Time may change our grief, but it won't make it disappear."[32]

10. **God never gives us more than we can handle.** Another cliché. How many times have you heard this? It has such a Biblical-sounding truth to it, but it's a lie. You certainly won't find it anywhere in God's Word. God allows us to have more than we can handle—not because He's vindictive and wants to hurt us. He isn't a God who metes out pain so He can watch us suffer under the weight of it. Our world is fallen because of sin. If we were able to handle everything that touches our lives, we'd have no need of God.

11. **At least…** Any sentence that begins with these words has the potential of belittling our pain and grief. *At least* you know where he is. *At least* you have other children. *At least* you're young enough to get remarried. *At least* she didn't suffer. The list goes on. It's actually a form of replacing the value and importance of our loved ones with the subliminal message that our pain and loss isn't nearly as bad as what others have experienced. It implies that it could've been much worse. Remember—there's no prize awarded to the one with the most horrendous and painful story of suffering and loss.

---

32. Clarissa Moll, *Beyond the Darkness:* Carol Stream, IL, Tyndale House Publishers, 2022, 31.

While we're on the topic of what not to say, I've also included things to avoid doing. Things like:

1. **Rushing our grief.** Since our culture views grief as a problem to be fixed, it's assumed that grief has to be resolved as soon as possible. This results in messages from friends, family, and society saying that *we need to find closure, move on, and let go.* However, grief isn't something we can resolve, nor is it something that magically disappears. It has to be experienced. It requires a lot of time and hard work. It's not a fast process, and it can't be skipped. It takes time to adjust to all the changes we have to make.

2. **Interrupting a griever talking about their loved one to talk about your own past losses and experiences.** When grievers are talking about their loved ones, listen attentively and avoid bringing your personal stories into the conversation. We need to talk about *our* loved ones, not *yours*. Chances are, we don't know your loved one. It can feel like you're comparing your loss to ours. We can't handle your grief in the midst of our own. Changing the focus of our conversation doesn't take our mind off our loss.

3. **Making a griever feel judged or evaluated.** Those of us experiencing grief are highly vulnerable. We're deeply wounded. So, having someone speak critically into our life is like pouring salt into a gaping wound. They, in essence,

are 'Job's comforters.' No one needs that in the midst of trying to navigate their way through profound sadness and loss. This kind of person is toxic, so it's best for the grieving person to distance themselves.

4. **Giving unsolicited advice.** When we share our feelings, it's not to gain advice or your perspective. We're airing our feelings because there's someone willing to listen. This, too, is part of dealing with grief. All we really want and need is to have someone validate the pain we've expressed.

5. **Being distracted by things**. If you're distracted by something (like your phone) while we're talking to you, it sends a message that what we're saying isn't important enough to give us your full attention.

I'm certain there are many other words and actions that shouldn't have been spoken or acted upon. I'm so sorry if you've experienced unkind or insensitive comments. As a young girl, I remember a sign in my dad's office that said, *"Put brain in gear before mouth is in motion."* That's wise advice. Remember, *"Those in the midst of grief have not only been hit by the bus – they get run over by it again and again."*[33]

Please be patient with us.

---

33. Gary Roe, Please Be Patient I'm Grieving: Amazon, 2016, 21.

Part Four

GRIEF

The Gift

The Gift of Grief

Chapter Fifteen

God's Call to the Church

Do not merely look out for your own personal interests, but also for the interests of others.[34]

This is pure and undefiled religion in the sight of our God and Father, to visit orphans and widows in their distress, and to keep oneself unstained by the world.[35]

It was my first Sunday back to church in seven months. I was no longer being accompanied through the front door into the auditorium by my husband. I had two new escorts. Their names were grief and sorrow. To say I was less than enthused about these new companions was an understatement. I wished I'd never met them! I wished that the circumstances that introduced us had never happened! I wished they'd go away! There was no negoti-

---

34. Philippians 2:4   NASB

35. James 1:27   NASB

ating how long they'd be living with me. Of course, they invited some of their emotional relatives to join us. I was stunned at how many there were! Shock. Denial. Heartbreak. Disorientation. Forgetfulness. Loneliness. Silence. Sadness. Suffering. Stress. Brain fog. Exhaustion. Insomnia. Vulnerability. Regret. Guilt. Worry. They all moved in. Shock and denial eventually moved out, but the rest stayed. They aren't ready to leave just yet. I learned that at least a few of them will be with me for the long haul.

So what made returning to church seem impossible? I grew up in the church; it was my second home. I loved the church. I loved the worship. I loved being challenged by God's Word. I loved seeing God at work in the lives of His people. I loved being involved. So why was it now impossible to go back? Instead of physically attending, I tried watching the service online, but I still couldn't engage in it. Why?

For me, there were a few factors. Perhaps if we'd been attending the church for years and knew more people, it *might* have been different. I was new to this church, and the idea of sitting alone, knowing few people and bursting into tears as waves of grief and unexpected triggers overwhelmed me, was too much for me to handle. Having an empty seat beside me where Ron once sat was more than I could emotionally withstand. When I was eventually able to go back, I tried to find someone to sit with, but that wasn't always easy to do.

One Sunday, I entered the auditorium and everyone was sitting with others and chatting. They smiled and said good morning, but then went back to their conversations. I sat in a chair with nobody beside me—no conversations to be had. I sat and prayed that God would have someone sit with me. I never felt so much like a fish out of water than at that moment. I could feel my chin starting to quiver, and I kept telling myself not to cry. It also didn't help that the one-year anniversary of Ron's death was coming up. I just wanted to get out of there. By the end of the first song, I picked up my purse and headed out the door. No one in the atrium spoke to me as I passed them. I couldn't get to my car fast enough. Once I got in my car, I sat there and cried. The loneliness was killing me as I drove home. I cried the rest of the day in the privacy of my home. No one called to see if I was okay. I felt like I didn't belong. No one seemed to care. I wished I could go back to my church in the GTA, but it was over an hour away. It's amazing that someone can feel so alone in the midst of hundreds of people. It can be debilitating for grievers.

Ron and I had always been very involved in the life and ministry of the local church. We were well-known and connected to others through small groups and various ministries. Ron was involved in building-related ministries like parking, the daycare board, and the building committee. Everyone knew who he was because he was on staff. I was actively involved in the music and prayer ministries, in addition to leading a large women's ministry. For someone who'd always been involved in music ministries, I couldn't sing for months after Ron died. I was so overwhelmed with sadness. Even when watching the service online, I'd turn the volume off and would just read the lyrics on the screen. When Jesus experienced deep suffering and pain, He didn't sing either, He cried. Another factor was that I simply didn't have the attention span or ability to listen. My brain was going in 50 different directions. Because of my brain fog, I couldn't retain what I heard. I felt like a child who couldn't pay attention to what was going on.

Clarissa Moll, whose husband was killed in a hiking accident, experienced similar feelings. She writes, *"A few months after Rob died, I logged into an online grievers forum and searched for posts asking the question I felt I could not ask my local congregation. I needed to know I wasn't alone. Did anybody else feel like they couldn't go to church anymore? The words I found amazed me… the answer was the same. 'I can't go back.'… Why couldn't I return to this place I'd once loved? If the church was meant to be a hospital for the wounded, why did my brokenness seem not to fit?"*[36]

I asked myself why many grievers say the same thing. In one sense, I was relieved that it wasn't just me who felt this way; however, it also caused me to question why this is more common than we realize. For me, it was loneliness and deep sorrow. My whole being was now dressed in a spirit of heaviness, while

---

36. Clarissa Moll, *Beyond the Darkness*: Carol Stream, IL, Tyndale House Publishing, 2022, 181.

everyone else seemed to be dressed in a garment of praise. I looked and felt out of place. My heart was in a place of mourning that desperately wanted relief and healing. It led me to ask, how can the church possibly help those who journey through the valley of suffering, death, and grief?

Most churches have a wide variety of ministries that touch every age group from babies to seniors. There are children and youth ministries, Bible studies, music ministries, life groups, evangelism, and discipleship training. There are support groups for the divorced, for those suffering with addictions, and yes, even GriefShare for the bereaved. This begs the question: Is a 13-week support group, such as GriefShare, sufficient for those who are grieving? What do we do when the program is finished, but our grief journey has only begun? How many people in the congregation are actually involved in a ministry to the grieving? The majority of those who attend GriefShare are not from the church, but from the broader community.

When someone in the church dies, there's an 'all-hands-on-deck' call issued. Family, pastors, and even some congregants are ready to help during the time of the funeral. Cards and notes of condolence are sent, and phone calls are made. People might stop by with a casserole or a dessert. Others attend the funeral and might visit or serve at the luncheon following the service. For about three to four weeks after the funeral, many are mindful of those who've lost someone—but subtly and gradually, life shifts, and everyone's attention reverts back to their own routines. Everyone moves on except the bereaved, who are left reeling from their loss, wondering where everyone went.

My friend Andy, whose wife died the week before Ron from a horrendous five-year battle with cancer, started attending a new church. He joined their GriefShare support group and found it helpful. Most of the participants were from the community, not from his church. Andy doesn't know many people in the church, which means they don't know him. Who would come alongside Andy after he completed the program? He shared with me how it's the loneliness that's so hard to deal with.

I spoke with a gentleman who lost his wife two years ago. He has family, but they live out of province. He, too, attends a GriefShare group at a church. He attends for the fellowship of being with others who are also suffering losses. He said he goes because he's lonely and he feels at home with them since they understand how the loneliness and silence at home are crushing for him.

I, like many grievers, found certain times of the day lonelier than others. For many, it's the evening and nighttime. For others, it's first thing in the morning. At times, the quiet in our homes can seem deafening, which only accentuates our grief. We then wonder if this is how it's going to be for the rest of our lives.

The grieving community has two things in common—loss and loneliness. Although everyone grieves differently, grievers have an immediate bond with each other. It's a unique community. We've all suffered loss in different ways, and although we cannot say, *"I know how you feel,"* we can say, *"I understand how painful this is."*

Do we go to church asking God to lead us to someone who needs encouragement? Do we make a point of looking for those who are hurting—who want to *fit in*, be noticed, spoken to, and integrated into the life and ministry of the church? Do we do something as simple as inviting them to sit with us so they aren't sitting alone? Our life is not our own. It isn't just about us. Our life touches everyone we come into contact with. This is how Jesus viewed the importance of coming alongside those around us, *"… to the extent that you did it to one of these brothers of Mine, even the least of them, you did it to Me."*[37]

When I spoke at Ron's memorial service, I thanked everyone for their role, big and small, in coming alongside our family. I made a conscious effort to point out that we were aware that the hardest days were now ahead of us and we'd continue to covet their prayers and support. Now that I'm alone, why does it seem so much harder to integrate into the life of the church?

Everything within me screams that I don't want to live my life without Ron. I hate being a widow! I hate the loneliness that surrounds me! I want him back! I want the companionship and security of his presence! I want to hear him say, *"I love you, Sweetie."* But I'm reminded of Ecclesiastes 3:1, which says,

---

37. Matthew 25:40   NASB

"There is an appointed time for everything."[38] It reminds me that God is present in the timing of all my concerns. Though I don't understand, my life is fitting into the purposes He has ordained for me. Since there's an 'appointed time,' I know He's never too early, or too late, when it comes to anything that touches my life.

During the first few months of sleepless nights, I cried out to God that I couldn't go through such intense suffering if there wasn't some good to come out of losing Ron. I begged Him to bring good out of it so He'd be glorified. I asked Him to use me to bring comfort and hope to others. He began to answer me as I read from Elisabeth Elliot's book, *Suffering Is Never For Nothing*. *"I'm convinced that there are a good many things in this life that we really can't do anything about, but that God wants us to do something with."*[39] That struck a chord in my heart. I prayed, "Lord, what would You have me do with this devastating loss?"

I knew I needed to be with others who've also experienced the shocking pain of death. I needed community, and I found it in GriefShare. It's the best way to avoid isolation, which is crucial since isolation brings separation. In community, we're safely vulnerable. But sometimes being vulnerable isn't always pretty. Sometimes it can be ugly, but in a sacred and holy way, vulnerability can be beautiful because it's deeply honest and authentic. When you love someone and they're taken from you, you grieve

---

38. *Ecclesiastes* 3:1   NASB
39. Elisabeth Elliot Gren, *Suffering is Never For Nothing*: Nashville, TN, B & H Publishing Group, 2019, 7-8

their absence profoundly. As one gentleman I spoke with said, *"Love is made to be the best, but can hurt the most."* This is so true. We grieve because we can no longer give and receive love from the one we've lost.

Conversations with people and attending the GriefShare program started to show me that the church lacks an understanding of how to minister to those who are grieving. Over and over, people I knew who lost a loved one expressed the same sentiment—that the church needs to understand and learn how to come alongside those who are deeply grieving. Yes, the church was there for some in the first few weeks, but life soon went back to the way it was, and those grieving were left to fend for themselves. It was during this time that God laid it on my heart to write a book about this.

The church has the opportunity, privilege, and responsibility to be conduits of His love and grace to the wounded. God has designed the church to be a community where grievers can receive the love and support they need. So, what tangible ways can the church assist those within our walls, as well as those in our communities trying to navigate their own grief journey? The following are a few suggestions.

Develop a Grief Team

This would be a team of men and women led by the pastor who oversees congregational care. It should have men and women on it who've personally experienced deep grief and loss. They should receive grief training before becoming part of the team. Their role would be to assist the pastor in providing support and care to those in the depths of loss and sorrow. These would be people who are considered 'safe people' who don't judge or give advice. They'd be there to support the griever by listening and praying with them. If the grieving person doesn't have any church affiliation but has an interest in attending, the team member would arrange to sit with them so they're not alone. For the first year of a person's loss, a team member would be responsible for quarterly visits with these people to comfort, connect, support, and encourage them. In the second year, the team member would follow up with a phone call every six months.

A Comfort Basket

When visiting a grieving person/family, taking them a comfort basket is a sign of support and care. The basket doesn't have to be big and can have any number of items in it. Suggested items might include Kleenex, tea, cookies, mints or candies, a photo frame, a journal and pen, or a gift card to a grocery store. Stephen Ministries has an excellent four-book series dealing with the first year of grief. Book one could be included in the basket. The remaining three books in the series would be given during the next three quarterly visits. If it's a grieving family, age-appropriate items for children could be included in the basket.

Offer a Grief-Support Group/Program

When people—especially from the community who aren't connected to a local church—lose a loved one, they often go online looking for help to survive their pain. There are many groups out there, but the vast majority don't offer the hope that's found in Christ. The GriefShare program is a doctrinally sound and Biblically-based program. It's considered the #1 grief support program in the world. People are desperate for hope when they've been crushed by the loss of a loved one and will often seek out a church for support. Those who lead GriefShare groups are people who've experienced the death/loss of a dear one, so they can relate to those who attend. They're also trained in the GriefShare program to become a facilitator. Personally, I received such deep ministry when I attended, that I wanted to become a facilitator to help others in their time of sorrow. A grief support group for children and/or youth might be something to consider as well.

Pastoral and Ministry Staff Training

Tragedy usually strikes when we least expect it. Are we prepared to come alongside someone in our congregation when it happens to them? It's invaluable for the church to have all pastoral staff and ministry leaders take a seminar in grief training. For instance, if there's a family that has lost a parent, would you, as a children's ministry leader, know how to come alongside that child? Like adults, children don't all grieve the same way.

"Research confirms that 'as children grow, they will need to re-experience the loss at each stage of development.'"[40]

A friend of mine attended a GriefShare program in his community, and there were two pastors that enrolled in it so they could learn how to come alongside people in their congregation and community. Their goal was to become facilitators and offer the program in their community.

Grief Seminar/Sermon Series

We live in a society that has an aversion to death and suffering. The majority of people in our congregations don't feel comfortable talking about death and dying, a reality that I've experienced firsthand. They don't know what to say, and are afraid they may say the wrong thing. As Christians, we should be the exception to this because of the hope within us. We should be willing and ready to show that we care. Consider offering a grief seminar to your congregation. Having a sermon series is an excellent means of addressing grief and loss. The whole congregation is there—young and old, men and women alike. I remember when Shauna and Brittany's friend passed away when she was just 22 years old. Her death sent those young people into a tailspin. When we're young, we tend to believe that death could never happen to us.

It's important that the person/people who deliver the messages in the seminar/sermon series have experienced

---

40. Clarissa Moll, *Beyond the Darkness:* Carol Stream, IL, Tyndale House Publishers, 2022, 144.

the devastating loss of someone very close to them. Textbook information isn't sufficient. So, if this requires bringing in a guest speaker who can relate, then do so. It's a worthy investment in the lives of your congregation. Involving some of the grief support group facilitators who've walked the journey of grief could also be considered as speakers.

Offer a Community Grief Education Day

The purpose of this day is to inform people of what's available in the community. Funeral homes, hospice, long-term care facilities, grief support groups, coaches, and professional counsellors from the community could be represented. There could be tables with information available for all attendees. Additionally, there could be breakout sessions with qualified speakers. If you choose to have a luncheon, you could have a guest speaker, followed by a question-and-answer time to engage the audience. The best part is that you can make this event as big or small as you wish.

A Grief Podcast or Blog

Today, people listen to podcasts and read blogs about every conceivable topic. Since our audience is the global world, this might be an option your church would want to consider, as it offers a broad and far-reaching influence in today's society. Reputable speakers could include clergy, authors, professional counsellors, and medical professionals, to name a few.

Incorporate Lament into the Church Service

The range of experiences that walk through the doors of a church is vast and varied. As I pointed out, many from the grieving community find it difficult to attend a church service for a variety of reasons. Simply put, lament is expressing our pain and sadness to God without trying to spiritualize it. Many of the Psalms are prayers of lament. It doesn't mean we've lost our faith in God. It means that we're going to God with our pain and suffering. It's an act that says how much we need God by being blatantly honest with Him. He knows how we feel and wants us to come to Him with our pain and sorrow. We all have painful experiences, regrets, and grief. As ordained pastor, Leanne Friesen writes, *"We need to give others this room to lament, as people and as churches."*[41]

Giving those around us the opportunity to lament enables us to stand with them. Lament can take place in the reading of God's Word, through prayers for the congregation and community, through the message, and through worship music. There are some beautiful worship songs of lament. We can take comfort in God's promise that a day is coming when He'll wipe away our tears and remove our sorrow, mourning, and pain forever. But for now, He stays with us to carry our burdens.

Host an Annual Remembrance/Comfort Service

---

41. Leanne Friesen, *Grieving Room*: Minneapolis, MN, Broadleaf Books, 2024, 151.

A church we attended years ago offered a special service of remembrance and condolence for family members and friends who had lost a loved one that year. The service was strategically held at the end of November on an evening when no other ministry events were taking place. The Christmas season is one of the most difficult to maneuver through because it magnifies feelings of loss and grief. There's so many triggers and waves at that time. Remembrance/comfort services should be about 45 minutes long; consisting of prayers, Bible readings focused on the Christmas story, the singing of Christmas carols and a brief 10-15 minute meditation. The church we attended at the time had a Christmas tree in the foyer with white lights on it. People took card-stock tags and wrote the names of their loved ones, the dates of their passing, and their names and relationships to the deceased. There was a ribbon on each tag so they could be hung on the Christmas tree. The tree was solely for the grieving, and it remained in the foyer for the entire Christmas season so that the congregation could read the names and pray for those grieving. Following the service, there were refreshments served in the foyer, giving people an opportunity to connect with each other.

Plan for Helping Grievers Survive the Holidays

GriefShare offers a special Surviving the Holidays event. Again, Christmas is often considered the most difficult holiday to get through without our loved ones. The program offers helpful tips and coping strategies. It comes with a Survival Guide book that features helpful articles to read and video clips featuring well-known counsellors, therapists, and pastors. It's designed to minister to those in the church and community who are dealing with loss, especially during this season.

In Memoriam

One of the things I like about my church is that on the first Sunday after New Year's, at the beginning of the service, they show a picture of each person from the congregation who passed away in the previous year. Their name and the date of their passing is printed under their picture. It serves as a reminder for the congregation to pray for those who are grieving. If you want to take it a step further, a page could be printed with the names and dates of those who passed away the previous year. The names of their families would be included to help the church to remember to pray for them throughout the year. Such a day can help remind people to encourage the bereaved with phone calls, notes, visits, or efforts to sit with any who might be sitting alone in church. It's one more way to remind people that death and pain are very much a part of church life, and that we need to support those who are walking through the valley of the shadow of death.

For additional ideas on how to come alongside the bereaved, see "Appendix A."

The Gift of Grief

Chapter Sixteen

A Few words to My Fellow Grievers

The presence of our loved ones is a gift to us from the hand and heart of God.

My daughter Brittany spent the day with me yesterday. It was my birthday. She planned a number of surprises for me. It was such an enjoyable and relaxing day together. We laughed, had fun, cried, and acknowledged how much we missed Ron. We spoke with Shauna on FaceTime and relished the little show my 17-month-old granddaughter, Haddie, entertained us with—playing "peek-a-boo" under a blanket, blowing a myriad of kisses and declaring oodles of *"I love ooo's."* I couldn't have asked for anything more. The best and greatest gifts were just being with them. It was about loving and enjoying each other's company. It was about their presence in my life. It was all that mattered and all I wanted.

As grievers, we identify with that deeply. At one time, we were with our loved ones, and we may not have realized it at the time, but just knowing they were present with us was enough. It wasn't until they were no longer with us that we realized just how important their presence was. Sadly, for many of us, we don't realize what we had until that person is no longer here. We so miss having them in our lives!

I adored my dad. When I was ten, I witnessed a dramatic change in his life through his relationship with Jesus. This encouraged me to tell him that I wanted to ask Jesus into my heart just like he did. He was a self-professed alcoholic changed by the transforming love and forgiveness of God. It was powerful! I have a copy of his personal testimony, which he wrote by hand. I'll always cherish it! I have the precious memory of him and my mother leading me to Christ on April 3, 1964, at 7:30 pm. The date, time, and place of that memory are forever imprinted on my mind and heart.

After my mom died in 2016, I visited my dad nearly every day in the retirement home and later, in the long-term care facility. I did that for the remaining three years of his life because I knew he was lonely without my mom. I couldn't imagine what that would be like for a 91-year-old man. We'd work on jigsaw puzzles, listen to old hymns on his CD player, or have the TV news station on in the background. Sometimes we'd talk about what was happening in the world and what a mess it was. Sometimes we'd reminisce about bygone days in his life and in our family's, recalling funny stories. Sometimes we'd look at the photo albums my daughters made for him, recalling special occasions. We'd enjoy coffee and cookies from the dining room. We'd often talk about the Lord, but I had no understanding of what it must've been like for him once my mom was gone. I just didn't want him to be left alone.

When he was in long-term care, he'd talk about how much he wanted to go to Heaven, but he questioned why the Lord wouldn't take him. He'd sometimes look up at the ceiling and say, *"I'm ready. Come and get me."* The week before he died, he made this comment again. I started to cry as he said that. He looked at me and asked why I was crying. I told him that maybe he was ready to go, but I wasn't quite ready to lose him. As only my dad would do, he gave a little laugh and said, *"Well I'm not gone yet."* He slept a lot in those last few days. I'd take his hand, and he'd drift off to sleep. I'd softly sing the old hymns he cherished. The last day he was in a comatose state, I took his hand and sang *"Tis So Sweet to Trust in Jesus."* When I started to sing the chorus, with eyes still closed, he smiled and opened his mouth as if he wanted to sing. I was shocked! When I finished the chorus, he closed his mouth. A week later, we sang that song at his funeral.

It wasn't until I lost my husband that I began to understand the sadness and loneliness my dad must've endured. He and my mom were married for 67 years. That's a lifetime. During every visit he thanked me for coming to spend time with him. He'd often say, *"I really miss your mother."* I'd say I missed her too, but I simply had no way of being able to identify with the depth of his pain and sorrow over her absence in his life… until now.

My dear grieving friend, only you know the depth of your sorrow and suffering. Those around you simply cannot understand if they've never experienced the loss of someone they loved with all their heart. I know, we as grievers, have sometimes said, *"As if I don't have enough to deal with in trying to navigate my way through grief, now I feel I have to 'teach' those around me what to do and what not to do, what to say and what not to say."* I know, it's hard. As I look back on my dad's story, I wish I could've encouraged him to talk about his journey with grief. Instead, I shied away from doing that because I didn't want to upset him and make him even more sad. I didn't realize that talking about it was part of the healing process.

As hard as it is, we need to share with those around us about grief. We need to help them understand what's comforting. We need to do this with grace, recognizing that before we were thrown into our own chasms of pain and suffering, it was difficult for us, too, to relate to or understand another person's journey with deep suffering and loss. We didn't know what to say or do to come alongside them, either. We, too, may have shied away from talking to them because we didn't want to make them feel worse.

If you feel that friends you were once close to have distanced themselves, you may need to talk with them about it. You may need to tell them how much you value their friendship and would like it to continue. Ask them if they feel uncomfortable with your grief. Be honest and speak with kindness. Let them know how hard this journey is, and that you value their love and presence in your life as you navigate your way through the unknown. Chances are, they're anxious about approaching you for fear of saying something they might regret later.

If you're unsure about something you're asked to do, don't be afraid to say you'll think about it and will get back to them. There's no pressure to give an answer in the moment if you feel unsure or undecided.

Try not to place unrealistic expectations on someone who offers to help you. Avoid asking them to do something that may not be their strength. My husband was always willing to help others—cut the grass, clean up, run errands, help move furniture, and so on. However, if you'd asked him to assemble a piece of furniture that came in a box, you would've seen a side of frustration like you've never witnessed before. Each of us has strengths and weaknesses. Don't be afraid to ask if they're comfortable doing what you're asking of them. We need to be mindful of not asking someone to do something they may not be capable of—or that they find frustrating.

Recognize that in some cases, the friendship might not continue. Everyone has people in their lives with whom they've lost touch over time. This doesn't necessarily mean the friendship ended on a bad note. As I write this, I've learned that a dear friend from my past died of cancer. We'd lost touch over the years. Ron and I moved an hour away, and our lives became busy with our jobs, our new church, our kids, and new friends. Her family was equally busy with their lives. Situations like this are just part of life. I plan to attend her funeral because I have fond memories of our times together, and it would be nice to see her family. The same happened at Ron's memorial, as people we hadn't seen for years attended in support of our family. It touched our hearts deeply. Just as there are different chapters in a book, the same can be said of different chapters in our lives with friendships we made over the years. The best part of the day will be spending time together and appreciating each other's presence in that moment. Who knows, there might be some reconnections made, which would be a gift.

I've said this before, but it bears repeating—the most important thing is to avoid isolating ourselves from being with others. Looking back on my dad's situation, the best thing I did for him was to be *present*. As fellow grievers, we know from experience how lonely we are upon losing 'that special person.' The days can seem so long because all we want is our loved one's company again. Maintaining connection with others safeguards against the danger of isolating ourselves, which is so important.

Being part of the grief support group was such a blessing in my life and in the lives of those who attended. We all said the same thing—we needed to be together. We supported each other. We understood how painful grief is and could identify with each other because we had that in common. The amazing thing about the GriefShare program was that, amid our own pain, we were able to reach out and encourage each other because we were all at different points in our journeys. At first, I was afraid it would be one big cry party, but that wasn't the case. Yes, we freely cried, but the bond of support was a true gift. At the end of the program, people wanted to stay connected, so we all exchanged email addresses and phone numbers. What a blessing and gift that was for everyone! We all look forward to reconnecting.

You can honour your loved one's memory by simply looking for a way to come alongside others. Our lives aren't meant to revolve around just ourselves, as life is about reaching out to others and blessing their lives. As we do that, we come to appreciate and enjoy the presence of others, which becomes a beautiful gift for both them and us.

The Gift of Grief

Chapter Seventeen

A Heart of Gratitude

I have learned to kiss the wave that throws me up against the Rock of Ages.[42]

… in everything give thanks; for this is God's will for you in Christ Jesus.[43]

When our children were young, how often did we try to instill in them the importance of saying thank you when they received something? We'd ask them, *"What do you say?"* They'd respond, *"Thank you."* That lesson applies to us in our relationship with

---

42. Charles Spurgeon has been credited with this quotation for decades, however, in researching which book or sermon it was recorded in, the search for this exact quote comes up short. In a Google search, a blog from the Spurgeon Center Library denies that Spurgeon wrote this quote. The closest wording to this is found in Spurgeon's November 1, 1874 sermon # 3115 entitled, Sin and Grace, *"The wave of temptation may even wash you higher up upon the Rock of ages, so that you cling to it with a firmer grip than you have ever done before, and so again where sin abounds, grace will much more abound."* The Spurgeon Center, http://center.spurgeon.org/2017/08/24, *Six Quotes Spurgeon Didn't Say.*

43. I Thessalonians 5:18   NASB.

our Heavenly Father. It's easy to say thank you when we get what we want or when things go our way, but are we as quick to thank Him for the hard times, the sad times, and for the sorrow that floods our soul? Do we thank Him for the unanswered prayers? As His children, do we also have to be reminded to thank Him? We need to thank Him, not only for His gifts to us and for answered prayers, but for the pain and suffering we endure. Do we express our gratitude to Him for walking with us through the valley of death, loss, and sorrow?

Upon learning that Ron passed away, dear friends of ours, Rob and Myrna, sent me Elisabeth Elliot's book, *Suffering Is Never For Nothing*. Rob was Ron's best man and Myrna was one of my bridesmaids at our wedding. They worked on staff at Bayview Glen Church with Ron. They live in Texas now, but when they heard that Ron died, they called and asked if it was true. It was shocking to so many people.

This book was such a ministry to my aching heart. At the onset of reading it, I couldn't take in very much because of the shock I was in. However, when I re-read it a few months later, something jumped out at me that I had overlooked the first time I read it. It's a paragraph I want to share because it was the confirmation I needed to write this book. Elisabeth writes, "... *Psalm 55:22, "Cast your burden on the Lord and He shall sustain you" (NKJV). To my amazement and delight I discovered that that word burden in the Hebrew is the same word as the word for **gift**.* (emphasis mine) *This is a transforming truth to me. If I thank God for this very thing which is killing me, I can begin dimly and faintly to see it as a gift. I can realize that it is through that very thing which is so far from being the thing I would have chosen, that God wants to teach me His way of salvation.'*[44]

Gratitude. How is it possible to be thankful amid the whirlwind of loss and overwhelming distress? How can we be thankful for the deepest pain of our lives? It's not easy. Many of us experience confusion, numbness, shock, and denial, not to mention the sorrow that's overtaken us. What is there to be thankful for? The love of my life is gone. The relationship is finished. I'm not thankful for that! I want him back! But over time, I learned a valuable lesson about gratitude. Gratitude helps to ground me. Gratitude provides a foundation of stability and calm when I'm otherwise feeling like my life is out of control. It gives my soul a much-needed, momentary reprieve amid the constant upheaval of painful emotions.

I purposed in my heart that I'd thank God for something each day. I was thankful I wasn't alone when I got the news that Ron died. I was so grateful that Shauna and Brittany were together when they got the call. God knew they needed to be together. I was thankful for those who assisted me with the preparations for the memorial service, even from as far away as Wisconsin (thank you, DJ). My sister and brother-in-law were (and still are) here

---

44. Elisabeth Elliot Gren, *Suffering is Never For Nothing:* Nashville, TN, B & H Publishing Group, 2019, 72-73.

for me day and night. My girls were and continue to be in constant contact with me, checking to make sure I'm okay. Close friends would check in to see how I was doing, which meant so much to me. I was indebted to God for the husband He chose to bless me with and for the time we had together. I'm grateful for the gift of so many wonderful memories.

Gratitude points me toward the hope I have in Christ. Thankfulness has a positive influence on my life moving forward. It reminds me that I don't have to walk this road alone. It helps build resilience as I journey through grief. It reinforces that although my husband is gone, I still have more life to live and I can do so in a way that honours his memory. Gratitude is taking my eyes off me and focusing on the blessings of others in my life and being a blessing to them. I've learned that I can grieve my loss and be thankful at the same time. I've discovered that gratitude is a transformative force. As I focus on my blessings, it brings healing into my life.

In looking back, I can see how the Lord used a devastating experience to bring glory to His Name. I see how a stranger in a parking lot, who told me to give myself the gift of grief, gave me an important message to pass on to others. I never anticipated the journey that would be mine in discovering what 'the ***gift*** of grief' actually is. Little did I know at that time how this stranger's words would become the title of this book. Never did I dream that I'd even be writing a book!

Being part of the GriefShare program was the next step of confirmation that this book was going to be written. I met others who shared their brokenness and tears of sorrow with me, and I with them. I became a member of a community that I would never have chosen. Yet, in looking back, I'm so grateful for this unique community of grievers. I continue to learn so much from them and want to share how Jesus has used this experience to deepen my faith and my love for Him. I want to help them as they walk their journey of sorrow.

I'm grateful because the Lord answered my prayers about where He wants me to serve in the church. I thought it might be in Women's Ministries, but He has shown me that He has a different plan for my life. I can see how He's using the gifts He gave me during my years of leading Women's Ministries to prepare me for the next ministry He has in store for me. It's just one more confirmation that He's in control of my life and will bring beauty out of ashes. He's taking good care of me, just as He promised me that first night, and will continue to guide my steps as I trust Him. He's confirming my life verse that was chosen back in Bible college days, *"And the Lord is the one who goes ahead of you; He will be with you. He will not fail you or forsake you. Do not fear, or be dismayed."*[45]

My heart was profoundly ministered to when I heard the phrase, *"I have learned to kiss the wave that throws me up*

---

45. Deuteronomy 31:8 NASB.

against the Rock of Ages."[46] Although I don't like the waves and triggers, I now thank the Lord for them because I recognize that with each one, as painful as they are, they bring me one step closer to my healing from grief. I can surrender to and kiss the waves because they throw me up into the arms of my Rock of Ages—Jesus. Again, this isn't something I would've normally been grateful for, but I've begun to recognize that they're also part of the gift of grief. I'm learning that God never wastes our experiences, no matter how hard or heartbreaking they may be. I can thank Him for not wasting my experiences, because even though I don't like them, don't understand them, and don't want them, He's using them to bring glory to His Name. There's a greater picture that I can't see right now, but I know I can trust Him, that there's a glorious hope that lies ahead. In that, I take great solace.

---

46. See footnote 42 re Spurgeon.

The Gift of Grief

Chapter Eighteen

Where Do We Go From Here?

Come to Me, all who are weary and heavy-laden, and I will give you rest. Take My yoke upon you, and learn from Me, for I am gentle and humble in heart; and YOU SHALL FIND REST FOR YOUR SOULS. For My yoke is easy, and My load is light.[47]

One of the most powerful and emotional Olympic stories ever told is that of Derek Redmond of Great Britain. He was going to be running in the 400-meter race in the 1992 Barcelona Olympics. It was the semi-finals and he was favoured to win, but halfway through the race, the unthinkable happened. He tore his hamstring. All the runners continued their race, leaving Derek behind. He was in excruciating pain not only physically, but emotionally. He trained hard for this and was running for the prize of the gold medal, which was now out of the question.

---

47. Matthew 11:28-30   NASB.

Medics rushed over to him, thinking they'd take him off the track, but Derek said no. He had trained and looked forward to this moment. He was determined to finish his race, even if he had to crawl the last 250 meters.

All of a sudden, a man ran onto the track. Security tried to stop him, but couldn't. It was his dad. He put his arm around his son. He told Derek he didn't have to finish the race, but Derek said otherwise. His father's response was that they'd finish the race together. They proceeded to continue walking the rest of the track to cross the finish line. His body was broken and his spirit wounded, but in the face of adversity, Derek pushed through. The crowd of witnesses in the stands were up on their feet as he finished his race. The applause and cheers were thunderous. It was even louder than it was for the young man who won the race.

What a powerful example! It's a great reminder that the race set before us won't always be easy.

There will be unexpected setbacks and hurdles too high to jump over, but we have a Saviour who runs to us, puts His arm around us and says, *"We'll finish the race together."*

Perhaps you're reading this because you've lost someone very precious and dear to you. Perhaps a husband, a wife, a child, a mother or father, a grandparent, a niece or nephew, an aunt or uncle, or even a dear friend. Perhaps your loss isn't the result of a physical death. Maybe it's a job loss, financial loss, a marriage breakdown, or a painful divorce. It may be the loss of independence or health due to a circumstance that's beyond your control. No matter the loss, they all create debilitating pain and suffering, and we're left trying to figure out if we can even make it to the finish line. We question how we can move forward. At times, we may feel paralyzed or ambushed by the hand we've been dealt. Some of us may experience anger and frustration. Others may feel isolated, alone, and confused. Some may feel the hopelessness and fear that can accompany loss.

What's your loss right now? Just as Derek's father came alongside him and walked with him, we too don't have to walk this journey of grief alone. Jesus extends an invitation to each of us to come to Him. He's a very present help in times of trouble, suffering, and hardship. We're reminded in Matthew 11:28-30 that He invites us to take His 'yoke' upon us. A yoke was a device put on the necks of two animals to help them work together to pull something. Farmers used a yoke on oxen when plowing fields. Being joined together with the yoke made the job easier and lighter, as it split the load between the two. Jesus used this word figuratively so those listening could visualize a picture of Him coming alongside them and sharing the burden of their pain and suffering. He wanted them to understand that He could help ease and lighten the burdens they carried.

Jesus is fully aware of what you need, my friend, and wants you to call out to Him for help. Give Him your sorrow and grief because He promises to help you carry it. He wants to help carry and heal your shattered heart, your unfulfilled dreams, and your broken relationships. He wants to give you the strength to carry on as you walk this unforeseen road as part of your race. You do not have to walk alone.

Perhaps you haven't experienced a loss so devastating that you felt unsure of how you could possibly carry on. Perhaps you're part of the church and you're realizing that there are several hurting people in your congregation and community. Maybe you don't know what you should say or do because you can't identify with the pain they're experiencing. Coming alongside those in pain isn't easy. Sometimes it can be uncomfortable. It can be messy, but God wants us to reach out to those who are hurting and alone. He wants us to be His hands and feet to a hurting world around us, both in the church and community. We need to learn how to come alongside those who are walking through their journeys of pain and suffering. He wants us to learn how to listen to and care for those with broken hearts. He wants each of us to be a friend. Can we do that? It's an investment of our time and love.

There are hurting, devastated people all around us, and we have the opportunity to be Jesus to them. He wants to use us to bless them and help them heal. May His Spirit move your heart to see the blessing you can be, but also the blessing you can receive through your selfless acts of kindness and love to those who are suffering.

Epilogue

For I consider that the sufferings of this present time are not worthy to be compared with the glory that is to be revealed to us.[48]

"Give yourself the gift of grief."

At the beginning of this book, I asked the question: How can anyone think of grief as a gift? Grief is the furthest thing from being a gift. Or is it? As I wrestled with this concept, I got a glimmer of hope, as the Lord brought the words of Isaiah 53:4 to mind, *"Surely He has borne our griefs and carried our sorrows."* Jesus has put my sorrows and grief on Himself. Since He carries my pain and suffering, I don't face grief alone with hopelessness. Grief + Jesus = Hope. Grief is a gift because it points me to Jesus! **Jesus** is the ***gift*** of grief! Grief shows me that I cannot possibly

---

48. Romans 8:18 NASB.

carry all the pain and suffering in this life on my own. For the first time, I realized that grief actually *is* a gift because it points me to the One who died on a Cross to forgive my sins and carry my grief and sorrows. I was never intended to carry them by myself. No one is.

We try so hard to understand why God allows pain in our lives, but we'll never fully know the answer because His ways and purposes are so incomprehensible to us. We'd have no need of God if we could understand His mind. We'd be lowering Him to our standards, but the created is not greater than the Creator. We need to trust Him. In Romans 8:18, the Apostle Paul longs for us to understand that the pain, suffering, and questions that besiege us in this life will have absolutely no importance when we see the perfection and glory of what He has planned for us. *"For I consider that the sufferings of this present time are not worthy to be compared with the glory that is to be revealed to us."*[49]

Although it may not make sense to us now, it will in due time. When that time comes, we'll give Him the glory He so rightly deserves. However, it's impossible for us to wrap our brains around this concept. Only a Master Designer could orchestrate it. So, instead of trying to understand it, can we receive this promise of future glory in faith amid our current emotions of overwhelming grief and sorrow?

We, the Church, have a huge calling. That calling isn't only to

---

49. Romans 8:18 NASB.

our fellow brothers and sisters in Christ, but to a lost community who don't have the hope and peace that can only be received from Jesus. When people in the community suffer the devastating loss of a loved one, to whom or to what can they turn in order to find hope? They desperately want it so they can get through the darkest days of their lives—be it the death of a loved one or the loss of a job, a home, their finances, or their health. We're to be an extension of the Master's hand to those who are suffering loss. We are called to come alongside the bereaved and be a gift to them.

Upon completing the GriefShare program at the church, the question that kept gnawing at me was, *"What do we do with those who have completed the program?"* How do we continue to minister to them? Do we put the onus on them to figure out for themselves how they can move forward from that point on? Some will return and redo the program because there's so much to take in that they can't process it all. Some will return because they long for the fellowship of this unique community. They've been in a group setting for 13 weeks, sharing the most painful losses anyone can experience. They've developed relationships with each other. They've been vulnerable in trusting each other with their wounds, their shattered hearts, and their tears. Is there something else we can offer them? This is a very important question for the Church to answer, especially in light of people from the community who have no hope but opt to seek help from the church. We need to learn what it's like to walk in their shoes. We need to learn to come alongside them in a non-judgmental way, offering a shoulder to cry on, a hug, and reassurance that we will love and support them in any way we can.

When people had physical needs, Jesus ministered to them. He took action and met their temporal needs. This gave Him the opportunity to meet them at their deepest point of spiritual need—their need of Him. It's time for the Church to start coming alongside and building up not only those within the church walls who are grieving, but also those who are grieving without hope in our community. If we don't know how to minister to the grievers within the Body of Christ, how can we possibly minister to those in our communities who are desperately searching for something to hang on to? If we don't learn, we will have failed them all.

There's always a purpose behind what we experience in our lives. Ultimately, in God's economy, it's to draw us closer to Him. Once again, I'm reminded that God never wastes our experiences.

I can now say, amid my ongoing grief and pain, that grief truly is a gift from God. Why?

- Because grief points me to the One who has willingly taken my pain and sorrow onto Himself, so I don't have to carry it alone.

- Because grief shows me that God is bigger than my suffering.

- Because grief has taught me that my identity isn't in the one who died, but in the One who lives.

- Because grief has taught me that God's grace is truly sufficient to meet all my needs.

- Because grief has taught me the value of living a life of gratitude.

- Because grief has shown me the faithfulness of God in my life and that He'll take good care of me, just as He promised.

- Because grief has given me a greater perspective on what really matters in life.

- Because grief has enabled me to connect with others who are trying to navigate the deep waters of loss to encourage them on their journey.

- Because grief has taught me that by focusing on others, I'm being healed in the process.

- Because grief has shown me that I can move forward with strength and confidence in my 'new normal.'

- Because grief has taught me that the end goal isn't about no longer grieving, but rather, showing me who I am and what I can be in the midst of it.

- Because grief has blessed me with the privilege of identifying with His sufferings.

- Because grief has given me the opportunity to share the hope I have in Christ on a deeper level with more people than I ever dreamed possible.

- Because grief has reinforced what's really important in life—relationships—with God and with each other.

- Because grief has affirmed my need to see things from eternity's perspective.

- Because grief has shown me it's only people that we take from this life into eternity.

As the Apostle Paul says, *"For our light affliction, which is but for a moment, is working for us a far more exceeding and eternal weight of glory."*[50]

God loves us so much that he willingly gave His own Son to carry the full weight and debt of our sin so that we can have eternal life. With that gift of eternal life, we receive additional gifts of peace, hope and yes, even joy. We don't have to walk through the valley of the shadow of death alone.

For those of you who are reading this book and trying to navigate your way through grief and loss, I encourage you to give yourself 'the *gift* of grief.' You were never intended to walk this road alone and I promise you, God *never* wastes our experiences.

---

50. 2 Corinthians 4:17 NKJV.

Appendix A

Additional Ideas for Chapter 15: "A Call to the Church"

1. Have a social gathering at the conclusion of a grief support program. *i.e.* potluck, brunch, BBQ etc.

2. Invite and accompany a griever to a church event, like a musical, Alpha, or the youth group/kids ministry if they have children.

3. Creative crafting group—help a griever to make a scrapbook or a shadow box of memories, a memorial bracelet, floral arrangement, etc.

4. Offer a monthly games afternoon at the church for grievers to connect and play games; like Cribbage, Euchre, Scrabble, etc. It helps to prevent isolation.

5. Start a weekly walking group and then go for coffee together after the walk.

6. Make a memory quilt together and then donate it to a women's shelter.

7. Start a griever's book club or Bible study. (This would be further on in their grief journey).

8. Go on an outing—i.e. a Blue Jays game, a bus trip to see the fall leaves/Christmas lights, and go out for dinner after.

9. Invite and accompany them to a concert or movie night at the church or in the community.

10. The arts—offer classes where they can express their grief and experience healing through photography, painting, writing, music, etc. This would require leaders who are skilled in these areas.

11. Offer seminars for community and church people—could be for a local hospice; or could be health related, self-care seminars concerning nutrition, exercise, or sleep. Offer a financial management seminar.

12. Create a home-helps team that could help with ongoing home maintenance, especially for widows. Members of the team could offer simple repairs like window cleaning, lawn mowing, leaf raking, snow shovelling, etc. Acts of kindness go a long way.

13. Invite someone over for coffee or lunch/dinner. It's hard for grievers to be motivated to cook for one.

14. Take a griever out for a drive in the country, or stop in small towns. Wander together down their main streets and check out some of the shops.

15. Offer to help a widow with her income tax if she needs help. Finances can be overwhelming and add tremendous stress, especially if she isn't used to looking after them.

16. Send a card or note by snail mail. People love to get mail. It shows they aren't forgotten. There's healing in reading notes. If you know of special dates they'll be facing, a card sent on or near that date means so much.

17. Make a phone call—a powerful way to encourage someone who feels down.

18. Offer to watch a single mom or dad's children for an afternoon (no charge). A break is a priceless gift to them. Offering to take their kids to and from a church program so the parent can have a 'night off' is a gift of 'me time.'

19. Assist single moms or take seniors who've lost a spouse to appointments if they don't drive.

20. Give a griever a gift card to a coffee shop, restaurant, car wash, or grocery store.

21. Bake cookies or cupcakes for a grieving parent who has young children.

22. Take a grieving senior a meal you've prepared for them. Better still, take two meals and stay to eat with them.

23. Offer to attend a grief support group with someone who's recently lost someone. It's hard to go alone.

Healing takes a lot of time. Faithfully pray for those who are experiencing loss. The silence in our homes can be deafening, so having the opportunity to be with people can be a gift to us.

Appendix B

With Personal Thanks …

The author wishes to thank the following publishers for kindly granting permission for the use of excerpts from their authors' books:

Exerpt from *Grieving Room* by Leanne Friesen. Broadleaf Books, 2024. Reproduced by permission of Broadleaf Books.

Exerpt from *Journeying Through Grief Book 4, Rebuilding and Remembering* by Kenneth C. Haugk. Published in 2004 by Stephen Ministries St. Louis, 2045 Innerbelt Business Center Dr., St. Louis, Missouri, 63114, USA. Copyright 2004-2-25. *www.stephenministries.org*

Exerpt from *Suffering Is Never For Nothing*, by Elisabeth Elliot, Copyright © 2019, pp 7-8, 72-73. Used by permission of Lifeway Christian Resource, Brentwood, Tennessee 37027, *www.lifeway.com.*

Exerpt from *It's OK That You're Not OK* © 2017 Megan Devine, used with permission from the publisher, "Sounds True Inc."

Notes:

Notes:

Notes:

Notes:

Notes:

Notes:

www.ingramcontent.com/pod-product-compliance
Lightning Source LLC
Chambersburg PA
CBHW061218070526
44584CB00029B/3879